"Brian Godawa is that rare breed—a
eyes to the aesthetic dimension of spi
read, this book analyzes the rich varie̜y ̣̣̣̣ ̣̣̣̣̣̣̣ ̣̣̣̣̣̣ ̣̣̣̣̣ ̣̣̣̣ ̣̣̣̣̣
ture itself. Godawa shows convincingly that God interacts with us as
whole persons, not only through didactic teaching but also through metaphor, symbol and sacrament."

NANCY R. PEARCEY, Francis A. Schaeffer Scholar, World Journalism Insti-
tute, and author of *Total Truth: Liberating Christianity from Its Cultural Captivity*

"At a contentious intersection of faith and contemporary culture, Brian
Godawa offers what many of us have been calling for: balance. In a world
(and often a church) torn by imbalanced devotion to either word or image,
Godawa joins the two with a needed 'and.' He shows a well-developed
literacy for both forms of communication, shows how the Bible incorpo-
rates both and challenges us to engage our culture creatively and redemptively on both fronts."

BRIAN MCLAREN, author of *A New Kind of Christian* and *A Generous Orthodoxy*

"This is must reading for anyone interested in the huge question of the use
of words and the legitimacy of images for theological and apologetic discourse. Brian Godawa has left no stone unturned. Moving insightfully
through the Bible, Luther, Calvin, Tolkien, Lewis and, of course, films,
Godawa lays to rest the many fears about images and imagination. More
than that, he encourages Christians to get involved in the media, with a
view to transforming them rather than hiding behind the safe wall of
'Christian art.'"

WILLIAM EDGAR, professor of apologetics, Westminster Theological Seminary

"Accessible and engaging, *Word Pictures* introduces readers to the popular
discourse among religious conservatives about visual culture in a mass-
mediated society. The strength of *Word Pictures* lies in the author's fresh explication of biblical passages, 'literarily' situating them in both generic and
cultural contexts and then drawing interesting parallels for thinking about
contemporary popular art."

WILLIAM ROMANOWSKI, professor of communication arts and sciences, Calvin College, and author of *Eyes Wide Open: Looking for God in Popular Culture*

BRIAN GODAWA

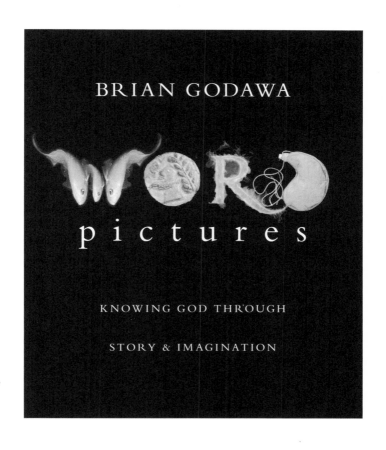

KNOWING GOD THROUGH

STORY & IMAGINATION

IVP Books

An imprint of InterVarsity Press
Downers Grove, Illinois

InterVarsity Press
P.O. Box 1400, Downers Grove, IL 60515-1426
World Wide Web: www.ivpress.com
E-mail: email@ivpress.com

InterVarsity Press® is the book-publishing division of InterVarsity Christian Fellowship/USA®, a movement
of students and faculty active on campus at hundreds of universities, colleges and schools of nursing in the
United States of America, and a member movement of the International Fellowship of Evangelical Students.
For information about local and regional activities, write Public Relations Dept., InterVarsity Christian
Fellowship/USA, 6400 Schroeder Rd., P.O. Box 7895, Madison, WI 53707-7895, or visit the IVCF
website at <www.intervarsity.org>.

All Scripture quotations, unless otherwise indicated, are taken from the New American Standard Bible®,
copyright 1960, 1962, 1963, 1968, 1971, 1972, 1973, 1975, 1977, 1995 by The Lockman Foundation.
Used by permission.

Cover design: Cindy Kiple

Cover images: Sharpfin sea bass: Ken Usami/Getty Images
          Flaming R: iStockphoto
          Roman coin: Albert J. Copley/Getty Images
          Sack: Jupiter Images

Interior images: ©iStockphoto.com

ISBN 978-0-8308-3709-0

Printed in the United States of America ∞

Library of Congress Cataloging-in-Publication Data

Godawa, Brian.
   Word pictures: knowing God through story & imagination/Brian
   Godawa.
      p. cm.
   Includes bibliographical references and index.
   ISBN 978-0-8308-3709-0 (pbk.: alk. paper)
   1. Christianity and the arts.   2. Imagination—Religious
aspects—Christianity.   3. Spirituality.   4. Postmodernism—Religious
aspects—Christianity.   I. Title.
   BR115.A8G59 2009
   230.dc22
                              2009011748

P 21 20 19 18 17 16 15 14 13 12 11 10 9 8 7 6 5 4 3 2 1

Y 26 25 24 23 22 21 20 19 18 17 16 15 14 13 12 11 10 09

For Kimberly

My godly and sexy wife

who has helped me to live a full life

of spirituality and sensuality.

And for Bishop N. T. Wright

A theologian of story who hasn't

chucked his rationality.

Contents

Desideratum and
Acknowledgments

A word of explanation about the design of this book. Throughout the text are embedded images that interact with the text and tell stories of their own. The images vary from photos to engravings, abstract to narrative, captioned to uncaptioned, all to engage the reader with more than mere illustration. It is the argument of this book that word and image, reason and imagination, must have an equal ultimacy in our understanding of God in order to properly reflect their equal ultimacy in the God-birthed incarnation and God-breathed revelation. A careful reader will not quickly pass over these images but take the time to "read" them as part of the text.

The careful reader will likewise notice that for the text of each chapter, a different font is used. This is intended to incarnate the unique theme of each chapter within the text itself—a modern font for the chapter on modernity, an antique font for the historical chapter on the Reformation, and so on. I hope this will help the reader to consider how the very art of typography itself influences the way we think.

If this departure from book publishing convention helps to make the point of *Word Pictures*, I am all the happier. If it does not work for you, I beg your indulgence of my attempt to stir your thoughts about something we usually do not even consider: the power of image to influence the word without us even thinking about it.

I want to thank the following for their help in making this book what it is: First, thanks to Kimberly, for her loving and faithful support, without whom I would not be writing or accomplishing anything in my otherwise pedestrian life. Second, thanks to the *Christian Research Journal* for rejecting the article that eventually became this book. Because they passed, I kept writing—and discovering. (They eventually published what became my chapter on Paul's Areopagus apologetic.) Third, thanks to my editor, David Zimmerman, for his patient editing of my pathetic prose. Special thanks to those who gave input on this manuscript in one form or another: Dave Bahnsen, Ken Gentry, Nancy Pearcey, Joel and Michelle Pelsue, Ken Tamplin, and my fellow post-yadayada *semper reformanda* coconspirators, Jack Hafer, Neil Uchitel, Andrew Sandlin and Goran Dragolovic. And special thanks to Jerry Johnson for recommending the title of this book.

And as always, special thanks to Joe Potter.

"Imagination does not breed insanity.
Exactly what does breed insanity is reason.
Poets do not go mad; but chess-players do.
Mathematicians go mad, and cashiers,
but creative artists very seldom.
I am not in any sense attacking logic:
I only say that this danger does lie in logic,
not in imagination."

G. K. Chesterton, *Orthodoxy*

"It would surely be much more rational
if conversation rather than dancing made the order of the day."
"Much more rational . . . I daresay;
but it would not be near so much like a ball."

Jane Austen, *Pride and Prejudice*

one

Confessions of a Modern

I love apologetics, philosophy and theology. I've pursued them for many years as a dominant focus in my Christian walk. From my first discovery of worldview thinking in the writings of Francis Schaeffer, through my hungry devouring of every book on defending the faith I could read, my Christianity has developed through the paradigm of apologetics, philosophy and theology.

I've learned a lot of biblical doctrine within the context of how it contradicts unbelieving cults and worldviews. I've come to understand the nature of the "faith once for all delivered to the saints" in terms of rational defense of its propositions. I've defined myself through systematic theology, which includes objections to false doctrines. One might even say I've been obsessed with apologetics and rational inquiry.

When I first sought a reasonable faith, I did the typical Evangelical thing in the 1980s: I read *Evidence That Demands a Verdict* by Josh McDowell and many other books like it.

I then embarked on a journey of attempting to memorize every archeological factoid that supported the Bible, every empirical verification of creation against chance and evolution, every rationalized harmony of every alleged contradiction in the Bible, every historical fulfillment of every prophecy, that I could. I even studied as many unbelieving worldviews as I could in order to prove the rational superiority and truth of Christianity.

Needless to say, this Herculean task was exhausting. Like Atlas bearing the world, I shrugged. I thought that if I could just marshal enough facts, answer enough objections, master the arguments for the existence of God and show how rational Christianity was, then unbelievers would be forced into the position of "accepting" Christianity because it satisfied the modern canons of logic and science. If I met the standards of skepticism, the skeptic would simply *have to* change his mind because he followed logic and science "wherever it led him."

Then I discovered original sin—or more precisely, the noetic (rational) effect of sin. I learned from the Bible that not only has all humankind inherited Adam's curse of disobedience (Rom 5:12-14), but all unbelievers actually know about God and his essential nature but suppress that truth through their wickedness (Rom 1:18-21). As a result, even their reasoning is futile, their logic corrupted, their understanding darkened by willful ignorance (Eph 4:17-18). Every part of man—heart, soul, body *and* mind—is affected by sin.

Biblically, people are not unbelievers because they suffer the lack of reasons, historical verification or scientific proof to believe. They are unbelievers because they know the truth about God and suppress that knowledge sinfully. The problem with unbelievers is not ultimately rational, it is moral. As in the original case with Adam and Eve, sin distorts man's reason as well as his will. The sinner uses sin-tainted reason (Eph 4:18) and empirical observations to rationalize a prejudice against God (Rom. 1:18); he does not use it to discover truth wherever it leads. As

Puritan John Owen put it in *The Holy Spirit,*

> That Jesus Christ was crucified, is a proposition that any natural [i.e., unregenerate] man may understand and assent to, and be said to receive: and all the doctrines of the gospel may be taught in propositions and discourses, the sense and meaning of which a natural man may understand; but it is denied that he can receive the things themselves. For there is a wide difference between the mind's receiving doctrines notionally, and receiving the things taught in them really.[1]

The noetic effect of sin chastened my faith in the power of reason, but it did not destroy it.

LOGIC AND REASON

In order to avoid apostasy, heresy and just bad theology, Scripture must be interpreted in context with other Scripture (Mt 4:5-7). The Bible may declare man's rational faculties as fallen, but that same Bible uses reason and logic all over the place. It's irrefutable.

I studied the Bible with this privileging of reason. I saw how Paul vigorously sought to "persuade" people to repent (Acts 18:4).[2] That means rational argumentation; the Greek word for "repent" literally means "change the mind" (Acts 17:30). I treasured the discovery that God exalts the search for knowledge and wisdom (Prov 1:7; cf. Prov 8:9-10; 9:10; Is  1:18), as well as philosophy rooted in Christ (Col 2:8). I even came to realize that God's own revelation expresses or assumes the primary logical laws of identity, antithesis and noncontradiction (Ex 3:14; 20:3, 16) so

---

[1]John Owen, quoted by James K. A. Smith in *Christianity and the Postmodern Turn: Six Views*, ed. Myron Penner (Grand Rapids: Brazos, 2005), p. 227.
[2]See also Acts 19:26; 26:28; 28:23; 2 Cor 5:11.

often it's not even debatable. The apostle John calls God the *Logos*, a deliberate echo of the Greek notion of the underlying logical structure of the universe (Jn 1:1). Jesus used logic (Mt 21:24-27), and if it's good enough for Jesus . . .

So the question I struggled over was: How could the Bible be so equally explicit in its affirmation of reason as well as man's sinful corruption of reason? Wouldn't those two cancel each other out? Is the Bible contradicting itself? Or am I misunderstanding the big picture?

The reconciliation of this apparent tension has been attempted by Christians in different ways throughout history, but the bottom line for me is that the Bible teaches both, so we must affirm both or suffer infidelity to God's Word. What follows will show that getting to this bottom line will not be a non sequitur leap.

PROPOSITIONAL TRUTH

In my pursuit of rational discourse I came to love propositions, especially logical ones. They seemed to be so clarifying, so neat and tidy, in my quest for discovery of truth and reality. A proposition can be defined as a statement that affirms or denies something and is either true or false. In an everyday sense, proposition can simply mean "verbal statement," but in a theological sense it refers to a form of communication of truth that stresses the way things really are—or the factual, objective reality of something. In this sense, a proposition is cognitive, discerned through the rational mind. A poem or a prayer is not propositional because it conveys subjective emotional expression rather than objective rational description. The phrase "God delivers his people" is a propositional statement, but the phrase "God deliver me," is an emotional cry for help.

Scripture contains propositional truth—a lot of it. Contrary to the claims of mysticism, God *can* be known truly and sufficiently through rational propositions; at least God seems to think so, since he used so many propositions to communicate himself to human beings. God is eternal, immortal and invisible (1 Tim 1:17), God is love (1 Jn 4:8), God knows all things (1 Jn 3:20) and works all things after the counsel of his will (Eph 1:11) . . . These are just a few of the hundreds of propositional truths about God in the Bible. When King David, the prophet Isaiah and the apostle Paul argue the irrationality of idol worship, they make propositional claims and use logic as a means of proving their argument (Ps 115:1-8; Is 44:12-17; Acts 17:24, 29).

BOOKS

I was persuaded that, unlike some Christian anti-intellectuals, God considers logic to be an important part of understanding him. I was delightfully enraptured to uncover the fact that books are important to God too. In both Old and New Testaments, God's people are shown to be, so to speak, "people of the book." Their spiritual connectedness to God is often linked to reading and obeying the *book* of God's Law (Neh 8; cf. Deut 30:8-10; 2 Chron 34:30). God enshrined his commands in a *book* that Moses placed in a holy location beside the Ark of the Covenant (Deut 31:26). Old and New Testament saints constantly appealed to "the book" of Scripture for verification of their truth claims (Acts 17:11; cf. Ps 40:7; Lk 4:16-21; Heb 10:7). When the apostle Paul defended his faith, he paraphrased Scripture *books* and quoted pagan *books* to point unbelievers to God (Acts 17). Noble-minded Christians compared Paul's teaching against *the book* (Acts 17:11). Indeed, the final form which God encoded his truth to us is in *books*, from Genesis to Revelation (Ex 24:4; Rev 1:11). Being a book-lover myself, I thought, *Me and God, we seem to have a lot in common.*

WORDS

The more I read, the more I treasured words, since books are full of them. And words are central to the Christian faith as well. The Bible, God's revelation to us, is written in words. God created the universe and all there is using words; he spoke, and it was (Gen 1; Ps 33:6; Heb 11:3). There are literally thousands of examples in Scripture where God uses spoken words to make his point to pagans or his people. In fact, "Thus says the Lord" occurs over four hundred times in Scripture. He chose to use *words* to speak to his prophets and apostles, thus legitimating words as sufficient vehicles for ultimate truth.

The existentialist theory that language is inadequate for true communication or connection between persons is simply not biblical. After creating the universe with words (Gen 1), God created man *in his image* (Gen 1:26-27) then immediately *spoke* to Adam (Gen 1:28-30). He then warned him, *using words,* regarding the danger of disobedience (Gen 2:16-17). Adam's first recorded activity is his verbally *naming* the animals (Gen 2:19), an expression of his authority, reflecting God naming elements of the created order (Gen 1:5, 8, 10).

Children of God grow in their relationship with God through meditation on his *words* (Ps 1), treasuring those *words* in their hearts (Ps 119:11) and reading those *words* (Neh 8). The gospel is typically proclaimed, in the Bible, through verbal preaching of *words* (Rom 10:8-17)[3] and very often defended by *words* (e.g., 1 Pet 3:15; Acts 17).

So part of my responsibility in mirroring God's image, glorifying him and proclaiming and defending the gospel is to be rational, use propositions, read books and use words. So far, so good. But something went wrong.

LOGOCENTRISM

Over the years, as I pursued an emphasis on rational discourse almost

---

[3]See also Is 52:7; Acts 8:12; 13:32; Rom 10:15.

exclusively in my spiritual walk. I noticed in myself a tendency toward reducing everything to logical debate. I became argumentative. Encounters with unbelievers and even believers would seem to always end in cognitive dispute.

And I became impatient. With such a heavy focus on studying logical and historical argumentation, one becomes acutely aware of just how illogical and historically uneducated so many people really are. Most people's beliefs—and their defense of those beliefs—

are so riddled with logical fallacies that it boggles the mind. Or rather, it *frustrates* the mind. Some of the more astute Christian philosophers I studied taught me to think about the nature of argumentation itself, as well as worldviews. The philosophical pre-

suppositions that everyone operates under are so often unexamined that when you do bring them to light, they prove devastating to such unreflective viewpoints.

I became impatient with people who parroted received prejudices, actually arguing that Christianity is superstitious while putting their faith in the fictional fantasy of *The Da Vinci Code!* So I would engage in rigorous debate with the unenlightened and proceed to destroy unbelieving worldviews like they were going out of style. It was like a genocide of unbelief. "So, you're a naturalist? Well, if you believe everything has a natural cause, then your own thoughts are caused by nature, which means your truth claim of naturalism is self-refuting." WHAM!

"So, you're a relativist? Well, if you believe there are no absolutes, then that is an absolute, and you're relativism is self-refuting." WHAM!

"So, you're a monist? Well, if you believe all is one, and that distinctions between things are illusion, then you cannot disagree with me without making a distinction between your truth claims and my truth claims.

Your monism is self-refuting." WHAM!

I felt like the Muhammad Ali of apologetics: Trample like an elephant, sting like a hive of killer bees. But I eventually learned that winning an argument is not always the same as persuasion; you can win the battle of debate but lose the war for a soul.

I started to sense that my approach to apologetics and theology was becoming dehumanizing. I was treating the human being before me as a mere carrier of a set of irrational beliefs that it was my purpose to dismantle into absurdity—all in the cause of "leading every thought captive to Christ." As much as I would claim that the Bible was my ultimate authority, I would be more focused on logical discourse and rational inquiry than on truth in its fullness of manifestation in the *person* of Jesus Christ. I lost sight of the fact that Truth is ultimately an *incarnate person*, not solely abstract reasoning (Jn 14:6). Reason, not God, was my ultimate arbiter.

I was now what I call a "mind-oriented Christian." I tended to reduce other Christians to their doctrinal commitments, judging their status before God based on my creedal scorecard. "Well, you did okay, eight out

The Good Samaritan, by
Julius Schnorr von Carolsfeld

of ten doctrines correct, but those two wrong ones set you back on the hierarchy of doctrinal knowledge. I guess I will tolerate you." Through an inordinate emphasis in my faith on logic, rational discourse, words and books, I had transformed my Christian faith into a rationalistic philosophy lacking personal relationship and imagination. I thought mere theologically correct belief about reality was the same thing as inhabiting that reality. Emotions were irrational and thus irrelevant, because as all good logicians know, the appeal to pity (emotion) is an informal logical fallacy, and emotions cannot be trusted. Never mind that Jesus appealed to pity to persuade people (see Lk 10:29-37). Never mind that the Bible presents our emotions as a legitimate part of relating to God (see Mt 9:13; 22:37). Never mind that God appeals to pity throughout the Scriptures (Jon 4:10-11),[4] not to mention God's own emotional outbursts of jealousy (Deut 4:24), anger (1

Christ Driving the Merchants from the Temple,
by Albrecht Dürer

Chron 13:11), bitter weeping and moaning (Jer 48:31-32; Jn 11:35; Lk 19:41), compassion (Lk 15:20), grief (Gen 6:6) and shouts of joy (Zeph 3:17).[5]

---

[4]See also Zech 7:9-10; Prov 22:21-25; Rom 12:20; Mt 9:13.

[5]Modernist Christians argue that such emotional expressions of God are mere anthropomorphisms (human traits applied to God by way of analogy), as if such scientific categorizing negates rather than reinforces their emotional content. This is a non sequitur. Of course God is transcendent and we cannot understand him fully. Of course God does not experience emotions *in the same exact way* that finite, sinful humanity does. But he experiences emotion nonetheless, and he uses those human traits and metaphors, laden with human emotion, as legitimate means of understanding him. If one argues that such anthropomor-

I began to discover just what was lopsiding my Christianity and my communication. It was my devaluation of imagination. I had become *logocentric.* I had privileged rational discourse as the ultimate means of discerning truth and neglected the legitimacy of emotion and imagination in understanding God. Reason had become a sort of idol to me. And it was not well with my soul.

It was like a war between word and image in my theology, and I had for all these years considered *word* as the good side and *image* as the bad side—or at least the suspicious side. I needed to relearn a biblical truth: we are not disembodied intellects, we are enfleshed spirit that includes intellect but is not reducible to it. Our faith is not merely an abstract philosophy or mental assent to doctrinal propositions, it is first and foremost a covenanted relationship with the *person* of God.

WORD VERSUS IMAGE

When I refer to *word* and *image,* I do not mean merely literal things, as in the words you are reading versus visual pictures you see. If we think of word and image as categories of discourse, the category of *word* might include words, propositions, books, spoken and written prose, preaching and rational discourse, among other things. The category of *image* likewise involves more than mere visual image. The word *image* is a root word for *imagination,* which scholar William Dyrness defines traditionally as "the ability to shape mental images of things not present to the senses."[6] So the category of *image* might include anything that

phisms of emotion are not really emotion, then one would have to be consistent in saying that all anthropomorphisms of God are not really what they claim to be, such as justice, compassion, care or love. All these human metaphors of God involve intense emotion that is intrinsically a part of their image. If God did not want us to understand him as having emotions, he would not have used so many emotional terms and metaphors of himself. If emotions are a part of the *imago Dei* in us, then the appeal to emotion may be logically invalid, but it is biblically valid.

[6]William A. Dyrness, *Reformed Theology and Visual Culture: The Protestant Imagination from Calvin to Edwards* (Cambridge: Cambridge University Press, 2004), p. 4.

engages the imagination rather than the rational
intellect. This would include visual images, music, drama, symbol, story, metaphor, allegory
and other forms of creativity.

An example of the difference between these
categories of word and image would be systematic doctrines versus theological parables
and metaphors; describing God as a rock and
fortress may involve the use of words, but it ac-
cesses the imagination rather than logical de-
duction or scientific observation. As Kevin Vanhoozer explains, "The as-
sociation of ideas in a metaphorical statement is the result neither of
induction nor deduction; neither scientific observation nor logical reasoning create metaphors. Indeed, metaphor subverts logic; it has been
called an 'intentional category mistake.'"[7]

Traditionally, *word* has been considered more intellectual and *image,*
more emotional. *Word* has been linked with abstract communication, *image* with concrete communication. If *word* is more cerebral, *image* is more
sensate. The writers of the *Dictionary of Biblical Imagery* define image as

> any word that names a concrete thing (such as *tree* or *house*) or
> action (such as *running* or *threshing*). Any object or action that we
> can picture is an image. Images require two activities from us as
> readers of the Bible. The first is to experience the image as literally
> and in as fully a sensory way as possible.[8]

Though imagery in the Bible is communicated through words, the
usage of words is evocative, not of abstract eternal truths of reason, but

---

[7]Kevin J. Vanhoozer, *Is There a Meaning in This Text? The Bible, The Reader, and
the Morality of Literary Knowledge* (Grand Rapids: Zondervan, 1998), p. 129.
[8]"Introduction: Defining Terms: Image, Symbol, Metaphor, Simile," *Dictionary of
Biblical Imagery,* in *The Essential IVP Reference Collection* CD-ROM (Downers
Grove, Ill.: InterVarsity Press, 2001).

of a world of image, symbol, metaphor, simile, and story. As the editors of this dictionary conclude, "the Bible is much more a book of images and motifs than of abstractions and propositions."

This traditional dichotomy between word and image is better described as a dialectical tension between *reason and imagination*. I will point out later in the book that images can be just as abstract as words, and words just as emotional as images. The real question regarding the comprehension and communication of truth, then, is not "Are words superior to images?" but "Is reason superior to imagination?"

Over the years this dichotomy between rationality and imagination has been reflected in the broader Christian culture. Some Christians have tended to be so word-oriwented that they border on rationalism and distrust the use of imagination, deeming it an idol tool of the devil's workshop. Meanwhile, other Christians have tended to be image-oriented, with a more experiential approach to their faith and a distrust of dogmatic reasoning as close-minded bigotry.

A look at table 1 charts out how this word-image dichotomy has created a division in the body of Christ.

Table 1

BIASES	WORD	IMAGE
Locale	Traditional Church	Contemporary Church
Era	Modernity	Postmodernity
Emphasis	Doctrine	Relationship
Basis	Reason	Experience
Mandate	Preach the Gospel	Live the Gospel
Priority	Content of Message	Style and Form
Communication	Proposition	Story
Pursuit	Truth	Spirit
Values	Rules	Freedom
Temperament	Rationality	Creativity
Reference	Books, speech	Film, TV, Pop Culture
Vulnerability	Dead Orthodoxy	Anti-Intellectualism
Risks	Legalism	License

Theologically, I located myself on the "word" side of the chart. I sought to understand where this split came from and how it had affected me, and I began to see that my Christianity had been unknowingly affected by the paradigm of *modernity,* whose origin is most often attributed to the eighteenth-century movement called the Enlightenment.

TWO

Literal Versus Literary

*I*n the 1700s, the European Enlightenment introduced a new paradigm of truth and knowledge that demanded a foundation solely on human reason (rationalism) and empirical verification through human sense perceptions (empiricism) to validate truth claims. Science and reason became the only possible "objective" forms of knowledge. Religion was relegated to arbitrary subjective "belief."

The premodern faith paradigm (trusting deity leads to knowledge and truth) had been replaced by a modern scientific paradigm (autonomous human reason and observation lead to knowledge and truth). The rationalist skeptic René Descartes (1596-1650), with his *cogito ergo sum* ("I think, therefore, I am"), became the poster child for a viewpoint that believed human reason could provide certain knowledge of truth, because reason was founded on unchanging laws of reality discoverable by reason. Isaac Newton (1643-1727), with a paradigm of the universe as a clocklike machine that reduced the knowable universe to

René Descartes

mechanistic laws objectively observable by scientists, became the poster child for the scientific side of the Enlightenment story. Eventually every field of knowledge would become a slave to this Enlightenment prejudice of scientific and rational "management" of reality. The "science" of culture became "sociology," the "science" of personality became "psychology." The so-called Age of Faith was replaced by the so-called Age of Reason. As author Stanley Grenz puts it, "This quest led to the modernity characteristic of the twentieth century, which has sought to bring rational management to life in order to improve human existence through technology."[1]

Isaac Newton

Christians followed suit, seeking to found their faith on neutralist reason and scientific examination, the ultimate criteria of Enlightenment truth. Grenz and John Franke illustrate this epistemic turn in the theologians of the early twentieth century, like Charles Hodge, who suggested that "just as the natural scientist uncovers the facts pertaining to the natural world, so the theologian brings to light the theological facts found within the Bible."[2] Theologians developed a more scientific study of God, organizing doctrines into systems, much like the periodic table of elements or taxonomic classifications of animal phyla. Conservative Christians reinterpreted theology's chief goal as uncovering theological propositions of universal truths and facts from the Bible.

Even as evangelical Christians fought against liberalism, many of them drifted into the same set of assumptions of modernity: Science and reason are public facts and provable; religion and imagination are subjective faith and private. So, to legitimize Christianity, we must

[1]Stanley Grenz, A *Primer on Postmodernism* (Grand Rapids: Eerdmans, 1996), p. 3.
[2]Stanley J. Grenz and John R. Franke, *Beyond Foundationalism: Shaping Theology in a Postmodern Context* (Louisville, Ky.: Westminster John Knox, 2001), p. 34.

prove it according to the criteria of standards provided by modern science, historiography and philosophy. In the early twentieth century Christian fundamentalism defended biblical literalism with scientific appeals to archaeology and empirical evidence. Proving the historic and scientific reliability of the text of Scripture began to eclipse the narrative of the text. In her book *Total Truth: Liberating Christianity from Its Cultural Captivity*, Nancy Pearcey argues that the outcome was

> what one historian calls "a schizophrenic conception of God." On one hand, "intellectual assurance came from the Divine Engineer," while on the other hand, "personal religious experience assumed the Heavenly Father." Yet the relationship between them was far from equal, for science had been defined as the sole source of genuine knowledge, which meant religion was demoted to subjective feelings.[3]

Philosophical naturalism was unwittingly accepted by Christians as the reigning method of investigating truth.

> First, the very notion that Christians needed a "scientific" exegesis of Scripture represented a degree of cultural accommodation to the age. . . . Moreover, the empiricist insistence that theology was a collection of "facts" led easily to a one-dimensional, flat-footed interpretation of Scripture. Metaphorical, mystical, and symbolic meanings were downplayed in favor of the "plain" meaning of the text. And by treating Bible verses as isolated, discrete "facts,"

---

[3]Nancy R. Pearcey, *Total Truth: Liberating Christianity from Its Cultural Captivity* (Wheaton, Ill.: Crossway Books, 2004), p. 307.

the method often produced little more than proof-texting . . . with
little regard for literary or historical context, or for the larger organizing themes in Scripture.[4]

Of course, much good has come from Christianity rising to meet the
challenge of modernity. Since reason and empirical observation are not
intrinsically fallacious, and are indeed created by God, they cannot in
and of themselves be against God and can in fact be useful tools. But I
would suggest that we have allowed modernity to shape our understanding of Christianity as well. And not in all ways for the better.

Hans Frei, in his classic *Eclipse of Biblical Narrative*, explains that before the eighteenth and nineteenth centuries, the study of the Bible was
predominantly narratively driven. That is, while believers have always
had to defend their claims to biblical miracles and doctrines, they nevertheless studied their Scriptures in the form in which they were written:
not as textbook dissertations of timeless universal truths but as stories
and letters written to the people of God at a certain time and place in
history. But in response to the Enlightenment attempt to demythologize
Christianity, apologists have spent millions of pages and man-hours
seeking to prove the accuracy of biblical texts down to the jot and tittle.
Does flat earth terminology make the Bible unscientific (Rev 7:1)? Was
the creation account an ancient attempt to describe modern Big Bang
cosmology (Gen 1)? Was Jesus mistaken in claiming the end of the world
within his generation (Mt 23:36)?

Rather than embracing the imaginative language used in so many
biblical texts, theologians and apologists began to distrust it. Frei ac-
cuses Bishop Butler, a major influence in this tradition, of increasingly
modeling biblical studies after "precision and sobriety, if not always the
economy, of scientific discourse divorced from immediate appeal to

---

[4]Ibid., p. 301.

sensibility."[5] The study of theology and apologetics turned from the narrative text to the factual event *behind the text*. It's almost as if the biblical narrative became eclipsed by the pursuit of factual empirical verification of the text; a modern scientific obsession.

> Religious apologetics of all hues presented one obstacle, and historical criticism another. Both worked to good effect in preventing the exploration of a narrative interpretation of the biblical stories. Both were of course deeply enmeshed in the question of the factual status of the narrated events. . . . It has remained an obsessive preoccupation of theologians and many biblical scholars ever since.[6]

In my well-intentioned pursuit of defending the Bible, I voraciously consumed these obsessively "factual" volumes. Many of them would often apply the rules of evidence in a court of law in order to prove the Bible.[7] I began to see the text of the Bible less in terms of its narratives, poetry and images, and more in terms of a legal and scientific deposition intended to withstand modern analytic scrutiny. Rather than seeing the text through *literary* conventions of ancient Jewish culture, I would tend to see it through *literal* conventions of my modern scientific

---

[5]Hans Frei, *The Eclipse of Biblical Narrative: A Study in Eighteenth and Nineteenth Century Hermeneutics* (New Haven, Conn.: Yale University Press, 1974), p. 52.

[6]Ibid., pp. 137-38.

[7]What I mean by this is that our rules of legal proof do not validate the Bible because they are derived from the Bible. You can't "prove" the source of a notion from the results of the source of that notion. It is the source (the Bible) that proves the derivation (legal concepts). For example, the belief in a God who orders nature according to his orderliness is what drove many early modern scientists like Galileo, Isaac Newton and Lord Kelvin and other Christian scientists to pursue finding the "laws of nature, and of nature's God." Our commonly accepted legal principle that the punishment should fit the crime is based on the Old Testament notion of "lex talionis," eye for an eye. So, if our scientific and legal procedures are based upon the foundation of a biblical worldview, then logically, one cannot deny that foundation without denying the edifice built upon it. Of course, this does not make our interpretations of science or law absolute, like the Bible, because our building can be flawed even if the foundation is not.

culture. I became suspicious of poetic metaphors and hyperbole, because after all, those are subjective and enigmatic and eventually lead to liberal discrediting of the Bible as mythology. No, the Bible must be primarily literal propositional truth, a textbook of doctrine more than anything else. Literary genre and convention in the Bible was an annoying distraction from the clarity of rational precision.

I thought that if the Bible says the stars will fall from the sky, then stars must literally fall from the sky or else I'm a liberal who doesn't believe the Bible. If the Bible says that the whole world will hear the gospel before Jesus returns, then by jove, Jesus will not set foot on terra firma until every single person in every remote corner of the world has heard the gospel. Otherwise I am a liberal who doesn't believe the Bible.

The way in which I began to realize that my "literalism" was really unbiblical "hyper-literalism," was through my study of eschatology, the "end times."[8] Through studying the culture of ancient Israel I began to see that Jewish culture is poetic and laden with imaginative expressions, not analytic and laden with scientific factoids, like we in the West now read things. I began to appreciate what theologian Abraham Kuyper explained as the literary nature of biblical revelation as opposed to "barren proposition":

> The rationale for the diverse literary forms in Scripture is that revelation strikes all the chords of the soul, and not just one, e.g., the rational one. This makes it clear that the historical doctrine of revelation is not the barren propositional one it is often charged with being.[9]

---

[8]One of the most helpful books for exploring the end times through the eyes of first century Jews is Gary DeMar's *Last Days Madness: Obsession of the Modern Church* (Powder Springs, Ga.: American Vision, 1999).

[9]Kevin J. Vanhoozer, "The Semantics of Biblical Literature," in *Hermeneutics, Authority and*

Take for example the collapsing universe imagery of Jesus' Olivet Discourse:

> But immediately after the tribulation of those days the sun will be darkened, and the moon will not give its light, and the stars will fall from the sky, and the powers of the heavens will be shaken. (Mt 24:29)

I had been conditioned to believe that this event, heralding the coming of Christ, must be hyperliteral or a "barren proposition," that is, stars will literally fall from the sky and the heavens will literally shake. Well, God may do miracles but he doesn't do absurdities. Stars are suns and are a whole lot bigger than earth. One "star" alone would burn up the galaxy, let alone the earth, long before it even arrived here.

Rather than try to reconcile current scientific understanding of stars with biblical apocalyptic, it is more biblical to seek to read the text through the eyes of that first century Jew who wrote it. And that Jewish writer was steeped in Old Testament imagery. So when I looked into the Old Testament to find where that imagery is used, I discovered that sun, moon and stars are often used symbolically to represent rulers and governing powers. In Judges 5 stars are explained as representing ruling kings:

> The kings came and fought; then fought the kings of Canaan. . . . "The stars fought from heaven, from their courses they fought against Sisera." (Judg 5:19-20)[10]

Another example of this obvious symbolic description of the fall of ruling powers as the "shaking of heavens and earth" comes from the prophet Haggai:

Canon, ed. D.A. Carson and John D. Woodbridge (Grand Rapids: Zondervan, 1986), p. 78.
[10]Other places where sun, moon and stars are symbolic of ruling authorities or spiritual heads: Gen 37:9-10; Rev 12:1-6.

Then the word of the LORD came a second time to Haggai
. . . saying, "Speak to Zerubbabel governor of Judah, saying, 'I am
going to shake the heavens and the earth.' I will overthrow the
thrones of kingdoms and destroy the power of the kingdoms of
the nations." (Hag 2:20-22)

The text itself makes the analogous comparison that God's shaking
of the heavens and the earth is a poetic reference to his overthrow of
thrones, kingdoms and nations.

What's more, this same kind of terminology of stars and darkened
sun and moon was used in several biblical prophecies to describe the
fall of governments and political authorities. Isaiah describes God's
judgment and destruction of Babylon and her rulers the same way:

For the stars of heaven and their constellations will not flash forth
their light; The sun will be dark when it rises, and the moon will
not shed its light. (Is 13:10)

As a matter of fact, when this prophecy was fulfilled and Babylon was
overrun by the Medes in 539 B.C., the sun, moon and stars did not darken.
But this is only a contradiction if one demands a modern scientific literal-
istic reading of an ancient Jewish passage that is obviously cryptic and
figurative of falling leaders. Isaiah describes the fall of Edom's rulers under God's judgment with the same kind of language, but he paints an even
more dramatic picture:

And all the host of heaven will wear away, And the sky will be
rolled up like a scroll. . . . For My sword is satiated in heaven, Behold it shall descend for judgment upon Edom, And upon the
people whom I have devoted to destruction. (Is 34:4-5)

When the Maccabees destroyed Edom in 100 B.C. in fulfillment of this
prophecy, the sky did not *literally* roll up like a scroll, and the starry hosts
of heaven did not wear away, but the rulers and nation of Edom sure did.

Opening of the Fifth and Sixth Seals and the Fall of Stars,
by Albrecht Dürer

Both Old and New Testament prophets did not misdescribe literal objects they could not understand like meteorites or atomic explosions. They were not describing literal astronomical events defying the laws of physics. In short, they were not writing scientifically or literally. They were writing *figuratively*. They were deliberately using *images they were already familiar with* to depict the serious nature of God's wrath about to fall upon a nation or people.[11]

The biblical description of the "earth-shattering" power of the New Covenant begins to mean something when we read in Hebrews that we have received an "unshakable kingdom." It is not a physical description of the universe shaking, but a figurative one of the permanence and victory of the New Covenant over all human authority in heaven and on earth.

> "Yet once more I will shake not only the earth, but also the heavens." This expression, "Yet once more," denotes the removing of those things which can be shaken, as of created things, so that those things which cannot be shaken may remain. Therefore, since we receive a kingdom which cannot be shaken . . . (Heb 12:26-28)

The replacement of the Old Covenant with the New Covenant is here described as God "shaking the earth and heaven," because to the ancient Jew, the covenants of God with his people are the most important thing in the universe. In fact, the Covenant was described in terms of creating the "heavens and earth" when God gave it to Moses after parting the Red Sea:

---

[11]For more biblical examples of this collapsing universe and earth shattering hyperbole used of the fall of worldly powers see Jeremiah 4:23-30; Amos 8:9; Isaiah 24:1-23; 40:3-5; Nahum 1:4-6. For an excellent book about the nature of apocalyptic imagery and symbolism in the Bible, a must-buy book is *Last Days Madness*, by Gary DeMar (Powder Springs, Ga.: American Vision, 1999).

For I am the LORD your God, who stirs up the sea and its waves roar (the LORD of hosts is His name). I have put My words in your mouth and have covered you with the shadow of My hand, to establish the heavens, to found the earth, and to say to Zion, "You are My people." (Is 51:15-16)

The Renewal of God's Covenant, by Julius Schnorr von Carolsfeld

The Old Covenant was an "establishment of heavens and earth," so when the writer of Hebrews speaks of shaking the "heavens and the earth" he is referring to the elimination and replacement of covenants. In fact, when the first Temple, the center of that "heaven and earth" covenant, was destroyed in 587 B.C., the prophet Jeremiah not only used earth-shattering images again, but described the event as if the entire universe was in need of being recreated:

I looked on the earth, and behold, it was formless and void; And to the heavens, and they had no light. I looked on the mountains, and behold, they were quaking, And all the hills moved to and fro. I looked, and behold, there was no man, And all the birds of the heavens had fled. I looked, and behold, the fruitful land was a wilderness, And all its cities were pulled down Before the LORD, before His fierce anger. For thus says the LORD, "The whole land shall be a desolation, Yet I will not execute a complete destruction. For this the earth shall mourn And the heavens above be dark." (Jer 4:23-28)

The Destruction of Jerusalem by the Romans in A.D. *70,* by David Roberts

With all this understanding of the Covenants being described in terms of "heavens and earth," and the destruction of the emblem of the covenant, the Temple, being the collapse of the universe, then the Hebrews 12 reference to God shaking the heavens and earth once more becomes an obvious prophecy of the destruction of the second Temple that actually did occur in A.D. 70. When the second Temple was destroyed, this was God shaking the heavens and the earth of the Old Covenant and replacing it with a new permanent unshakable kingdom covenant that will remain forever.

So we see that all this biblical talk of quaking mountains, darkening skies, new heavens and a new earth is simply powerful figurative imagery used to depict the spiritual importance of the Covenants, both Old and New, not some literal physical phenomena of which we have no historical recording. That is the power of imagery. As New Testament scholar N. T. Wright explains,

> We do this all the time ourselves. I have often pointed out to students that to describe the fall of the Berlin Wall, as one well might, as an "earth-shattering event" might perhaps lead some future historian, writing in the *Martian Journal of Early European Studies* to hypothesize that an earthquake caused the collapse of the Wall, leading to both sides realizing they could live together after all. A good many of apocalyptic literature in our own century operate on about that level of misunderstanding.[12]

There are of course many straightforward descriptions in the Bible of historical events, but they are often interwoven with these imaginative images that help us understand the spiritual reality or meaning behind the event, because imagery has a way of picturing truth that abstract rational language does not.

A WHOLE LOT MORE BUNCH OF HYPERBOLE

Another example of the role of imagination in Scripture can be illustrated in the "Great Tribulation" that Jesus predicted in his Olivet Discourse. "For then there will be a great tribulation, such as has not occurred since the beginning of the world until now, nor ever will" (Mt

---

[12]N. T. Wright, *The New Testament and the People of God* (Minneapolis: Fortress, 1992), p. 282.

24:21). Prophecy pundits focus on the extremity of this pronouncement as proof of its future fulfillment. Surely we have not seen the kind of tribulation in history that is without equal. Yet in the Old Testament, the prophet Joel describes judgment upon Israel during his lifetime:

> Surely it is near, A day of darkness and gloom, A day of clouds and thick darkness. As the dawn is spread over the mountains, So there is a great and mighty people; *There has never been anything like it, Nor will there be again after it To the years of many generations.* (Joel 2:2, emphasis added)

Elsewhere in the Old Testament, when Nebuchadnezzar besieged Jerusalem during the prophet Ezekiel's era, God describes a tribulation that is very similar to the one described in the Olivet Discourse:

> *I will do among you what I have not done, and the like of which I will never do again.* Therefore, fathers will eat their sons among you, and sons will eat their fathers; for I will execute judgments on you and scatter all your remnant to every wind. (Ezek 5:9-10, emphasis added)

This destruction, which included cannibalism and a Diaspora of Jews, Scripture says God "will never do again." That makes at least three different times in the Bible (Ezekiel, Joel, Matthew) where Israel is described as being surrounded by pagan armies, and suffering great tribulation and desolations including a Diaspora. And each time is spoken of *as if it has never happened like this and would never happen again like this.*

But in A.D. 70, when Jerusalem was surrounded by Roman armies, Israel suffered a very similar fate as they did in Ezekiel's time: the people were starved and forced into cannibalism, and scattered to every wind in a Diaspora. Of this event the Jewish historian Flavius Josephus, reflecting good Jewish hyperbole, says,

The war which the Jews made with the Romans *hath been the*

greatest of all those, not only that have been in our times, but, in a man-
ner, of those that were ever heard of.[13]

Accordingly, the multitude of those that therein perished *ex-*
ceeded all the destructions that either men or God ever brought upon the
world.[14]

Josephus' writings may not be Scripture, but they certainly illustrate
the kind of hyperbolic language ancient Jews tended to use, which mirrors the language used in the Bible

Biblical apologists run verbal circles around themselves trying to
justify these statements as literal claims rather than literary exaggera-
tions. Why? Because literalism requires exact scientific precision. But
the ancient Jews were not applying these modern constraints to their

Bas relief from the Arch of Titus, Rome,
depicting the triumphal procession after the
destruction of Jerusalem, A.D. 70

premodern literature. They weren't contradicting themselves. They
were speaking hyperbolically to stress the seriousness of the issue.
The Scriptures are full of imaginative hyperbole that defies modern-

[13]Josephus *Wars of the Jews* Preface, Section 1.
[14]Josephus *Wars* 6:9:4.

ist reason. For example, two kings are spoken of as men of unique trust in God.

> [Hezekiah] trusted in the LORD, the God of Israel; so that after him there was *none like him* among all the kings of Judah, *nor among those who were before him.* (2 Kings 18:5, emphasis added)

> *Before* [Josiah] *there was no king like him* who turned to the LORD with all his heart . . . *nor did any like him arise after him.* (2 Kings 23:25, emphasis added)

These two men of God are very much like each other in their unique trust in God. If you take the Bible *literally* in all its writing, you must conclude that the Bible contradicts itself. But not if you understand it *literarily.* In fact, Solomon is described in a similar way:

> Behold, I have given you a wise and discerning heart, so that there has been *no one like you before you, nor shall one like you arise after you.* (1 Kings 3:12, emphasis added)

And this Scripture is "literally" contradicted by Jesus in reference to himself: "Something greater than Solomon is here" (Mt 12:42).

Well, was Jesus greater than Solomon or was he not? Which is right, the Old Testament or the New? Who is more trusting of God—Hezekiah or Josiah? Which of the similar Tribulations are the greatest? All these alleged contradictions become irrelevant when one sees the literary exaggeration that is going on here.

Exaggeration is not lying when it takes the form of a colloquial saying that expresses the emotional intent of the author. The biblical writers are ancient Jews expressing strong emotional images of destruction, faith and greatness, not geological, astronomical, empirical measurements. Those statements are not *literally* true because they were not *intended* to be literally true. And their readers knew it.

The Bible is simply full of this kind of hyperbole, especially in the apocalyptic writings of the prophets. The *Dictionary of Biblical Imagery* clarifies again:

> The events described in apocalyptic literature are often presented with literary techniques found more commonly in poetry: metaphor, hyperbole, personification, irony, numerical patterns and so forth. These special effects allowed apocalyptic to describe heaven and the future with captivating imagery . . . more like an impressionistic painting than like a photograph in high resolution. Individual details remained a puzzle, but the big picture was clear.[15]

Hyperbole does not reduce the Scriptures to fairy tales or unhistorical documents. Rather, it is an understanding of how God interweaves image with word to paint a picture of truth that retains an element of mystery beyond human rational reductionism.

> While the Bible is a very realistic book, rooted in actual, everyday events set in space-time history, there is also much about it that is fantastic. . . . The Bible seems to flaunt the element of fantasy by tending toward a rhetoric of hyperbole—the exaggerated statement that conveys heightened feeling in an obviously nonliteral form. "A thousand may fall at your side, ten thousand at your right hand," says the poet (Ps 91:7 RSV) in a heightened picture of battlefield deliverance. Again, "You will tread on the lion and the adder" (Ps 91:13 RSV). Similarly, the exultant confidence of David is so strong that he boasts that in God he "can crush a troop" and "leap over a wall" (Ps 18:29 RSV). The truth this hyperbolic rhetoric conveys is not literal or factual truth but emotional truth. The resulting spirit is exultant and buoyant, but it is not literal.[16]

[15]"Genre of Apocalypse: Understanding Apocalyptic," in *Dictionary of Biblical Imagery*, AGES Software.
[16]"Rhetorical Patterns: Rhetoric of Make-Believe," in *Dictionary of Biblical Imagery*, AGES Software.

Literary critic Northrop Frye correctly points out the irony that the meaning behind our colloquialism "gospel truth" implies veridical historical factuality, and yet the very last "gospel truth" uttered in the closing of the Gospel of John is a "dazzling hyperbole" of "intentional exaggeration":

> And there are also many other things which Jesus did, which if they were written in detail, I suppose that even the world itself would not contain the books that would be written. (Jn 21:25)[17]

The reader can only smile at the humorous irony of imagining modern apologists calculating the number of seconds and minutes in Jesus' life from birth to death and resurrection, then translating those segments of time into page counts, all in order to prove that Jesus' thirty three years of actions in fact could not be contained in all the books in the world at that time. Or perhaps they would try to make the ridiculous argument that since Jesus exists eternally, his history would require an infinite amount of books. The fact is that this gospel claim is not scientifically or historically true because hyperbole *is not intended to be a scientific or historical claim in the first place!*

ROLE REVERSAL

Because of the Bible's mixture of the literal with the figurative, the Bible student must be careful to consider the possible "literalness" of what may appear to be figurative language. The very success and growth of the discipline of archeology derives from the pursuit of men who refused to believe that the Bible was unhistorical myth or fanciful folktales. The history of science is filled with Christians like Matthew Maurey, the founder of modern oceanography, who interpreted apparently poetic Bible passages literally in a way that led to such scientific discov-

---

[17]Northrop Frye, *The Great Code: The Bible and Literature* (New York: Harcourt Brace Jovanovitch, 1981), p. 54.

eries as ocean currents (Ps 8:8; Is 43:16), the hydrologic cycle (Eccles 1:7; Job 36:27-28), the jet stream (Eccles 1:6) and air pressure (Job 28:25), to name a few.[18]

The Bible is so rich with integrated poetic *and* literal imagery that we should all be cautious about "eisegeting" our own bias into the text. If "exegesis" means drawing information out of the text of Scripture, then "eisegesis" means importing information into the text. There is simply no wooden or absolute hermeneutic of "literalness" or "figurativeness" that can do justice to the text. Context helps determine usage, but even context can be difficult to decipher. Literary interpretation of the Bible is not so much a science as an art.

One of the reasons why the Jews of the first century did not recognize the visitation of their own Messiah was because even *they* took the Bible too literally. Indeed, they were expecting a military or political king who would crush Rome (Dan 2:44-45), restore the nation of Israel back from exile into their land (Zeph 3:14-20), build a new kingdom on earth (Dan 7:14) from Mount Zion in Jerusalem (Is 52), rebuild the Temple (Ezek 40—48), reinstate the Davidic monarchy (Ps 89:38-51) in a new "age to come" (Is 61)—all based on Old Testament prophecy. Even Jesus' own disciples misunderstood the literary nature of these promises as literal earthly political power (Mt 20:20-28; Acts 1:6). Jesus' kingdom *did* crush Rome, though not through military revolution, Jesus *did* restore Israel, *did* rebuild the Temple (Acts 15:14-16), *did* reinstate the Davidic monarchy (Lk 1:32), and he *is* the King of kings who came to Mount Zion (Mt 21:5) and rules over all things at the right hand of his father (1 Pet. 3:22).[19] He just didn't do those things in the literal way that they had envisioned, but in a *literary* way. We see how the *literary* mean-

---

[18]Inspired by an email discussion with Nancy Pearcey. For an interesting documentation on Matthew Maurey, see <www.bible.ca/tracks/matthew-fontaine-maury-pathfinder-of-sea-ps8.htm>.

[19]N. T. Wright, *Jesus and the Victory of God* (Minneapolis: Fortress, 1996), pp. 205, 219, 223, 477-539.

ing of Israel and the Temple was first fulfilled in Christ and is now fulfilled in the church as his "body" (Rom 2:28-29; Eph 2:19-22). Christ's
rule in his kingdom may be current and real, but certainly not an earthly
reign of outward political power (Lk 17:20-21).

New Testament scholar Mark Allan Powell explains that the Gospel
narratives deliberately lampoon believers who are literally minded. The
Gospel of John alone illustrates many examples of literalizing "missings
of the boat": Nicodemus misunderstanding spiritual rebirth as *literally*
re-entering a mother's womb (Jn 3:4); disciples thinking that Lazarus is
literally taking a nap, when Jesus uses sleep as a metaphor for death (Jn
11:12); the disciples thinking Jesus has someone *literally* sneaking him
provisions when he says, "I have food that you know not of" (Jn 4:33);
and even grossly misconstruing Christ's Eucharistic reference to *literal*
cannibalism (Jn 6:51-52)! Powell affirms the conclusion that these fre-
quent misunderstandings are intended to teach the reader how to read
the Gospel correctly; not a wooden literalism but a literary narrative of
symbolism, metaphor, image *and* history all rolled up into one.[20] This
literary complexity may not satisfy the strict literalist who demands
precise categories and simple answers, but it's the God's-honest truth.

Even though they consider God's Word to be absolute and eternal in
its authority, New Testament authors, *writing with God's authority*, often
do not quote Old Testament Scriptures verbatim but rather paraphrase
them (Rom 11:8-10), allegorize them (Gal 4:21-31), typologize them
(Rom 5:14), quote from an imperfect Greek translation (the Septuagint)
rather than the more carefully assembled Hebrew originals (the Maso-
retic texts), quote using a mixture of Hebrew original and Greek translation (Jn 10:34) and from unknown translations that vary from both
Greek and Hebrew (Mt 4:7).[21] Biblical authors did not believe that a

---

[20]Mark Allan Powell, *What Is Narrative Criticism?* (Minneapolis: Fortress, 1990), p. 28.
[21]Walter C. Kaiser Jr., *The Uses of the Old Testament in the New* (Chicago: Moody Press, 1985),
    pp. 4-5.

The Woman Clothed with the Sun, and the
Seven-Headed Demon from Revelation, by Albrecht Dürer

scientific, word-for-word exactitude was necessary for an understanding of Scripture as God's authoritative word. *Literary* is not necessarily *literal*.

Biblically, the impact of imagery on the human audience is exaggerated, fantastic, nonliteral, dramatic, visual, experiential, emotional—and just as true as any of the historical, literal, abstract or rational propositions and words contained in those same pages. In its poetry, prophecy and proclamation, this mixture of word and image, rationality and imagination is so intertwined that even those in the first century had difficulty interpreting it! You simply cannot scientifically exegete the Scriptures as if it is a textbook of scientific facts or culturally transcendent doctrines or "objective" historical reporting. Biblical interpretation requires an aesthetic exegesis that takes into account the literary genre and artistic nature of the text.

Many Christians tend to impose a modern scientific standard upon their understanding of the Bible, an ancient Middle Eastern sacred text. They seem to be preoccupied with "the Bible as a true picture of the facts in all spheres of knowledge, secular, as well as religious."[22] Interestingly, this understanding began with Princeton theologians, such as Charles Hodge and B. B. Warfield, who sought to defend the Bible against "modernist" attacks in the nineteenth century. In seeking to meet the standards developed by atheistic scientific discourse, they unwittingly subordinated the Scriptures to those standards. Since then, the Bible has been reinterpreted to be in agreement with every fashionable scientific theory from evolution to the Big Bang and every fleeting literary theory from form criticism to deconstruction.

But scientific theories have changed so many times and with such drastic difference that a scientific approach to Scripture has actually proven to be historically fallacious. Those Christians desperately seeking to make the Bible "reveal" the Big Bang, for example, may eventually

---

[22]Carl Raschke, *The Next Reformation: Why Evangelicals Must Embrace Postmodernity* (Grand Rapids: Baker Academic, 2004), p. 125.

discover themselves as discredited in their faith as the Christians before Galileo who wed their biblical interpretation to Aristotelian science. "Whoever marries the spirit of the age in one generation," the saying goes, "becomes a widow in the next." Our understanding of a "scientifically accurate" description of reality is a historically new construct that could not have been in the minds of the biblical writers. They were not intending a scientific physical description of reality *in our modern sense of the words.* They were speaking within their cultural literary conventions of something beyond words. Neither did the biblical writers use these cultural conventions while secretly knowing the general theory of relativity. That too is an unfair projection of our modern viewpoint back onto their culture.

As Kevin Vanhoozer concludes " 'Error' is . . . a context-dependent notion. If I do not claim scientific exactitude or technical precision, it would be unjust to accuse me of having erred."[23] The Bible is without scientific error because it intends to describe reality not in scientifically precise terms *but in cultural or literary terms.*

Does this kind of imaginative interpretation start a person on the slippery slope of liberal mythologizing of everything in the Bible, including miracles? Hardly. If that were the case, then the biblical writers themselves would have to be called liberals; they were the ones who used imaginative hyperbole and exaggeration so liberally. But allowing for imaginative interpretation does make things a little harder to compartmentalize into evangelical boxes of settled answers and rational certainties. The fact that some things in Scripture are figurative and some literal are functions of literary genres and techniques, not scientific and rationalistic analysis. It may make the process of interpretation more difficult, but difficulty is not an argument against the truth of a belief.

In my fear of becoming "liberal," and in my overemphasis on the ra-

---

[23]Kevin Vanhoozer, *The Inerrancy of Scripture,* accessed February 5, 2008, at <www.episcopa lian.org/efac/articles/inerrancy.htm>.

tional, I discovered that I had been interpreting the Bible in a way that it was not intended to be interpreted. *Literalism* has become a code word for reducing Biblical language to raw physical description or rational timeless truths, rather than allowing for the imaginative poetic language of a Jew situated within the ancient Middle East. Yes, there is much in the Bible that is historical realism, much that is *literally* true, but it is mixed in with so much imagery, hyperbole and symbol that I simply can no longer claim to read the Bible *literally*. Instead, I've come to read the Book "literarily."

three

word versus image

In addition to being a lover of the mind, I am also a visual and dramatic artist. I love imagination and creativity. But in my pursuit of spirituality, knowledge, reality, truth and persuasion—because of my unbalanced word-orientation—my imagination was relegated to second-class status.

Here I was, an artist by inclination, training and profession, and yet the very concept of "image" was suspicious to me because of the propositional orientation of my faith. I didn't think the art that came from my intuition, my emotions or my imagination was necessarily *sinful,* it was just *inferior.* Images weren't intrinsically evil, but they *were* dangerous, like playing with matches, or better yet, like playing with a loaded gun. And why? Because they depended too much on emotion. And emotions were "irrational." And irrationality was the enemy of rationality.

Like a good evangelical Christian, I lamented our visual media-saturated society. I grieved with Neil Postman that we were "amusing ourselves to death"; media like television had replaced the reliability of words and rational discourse with the unreliable manipulation of visual images and emotional expression. I assumed that my emphasis on reason, propositional truth, words and books was simply an objective biblical paradigm.

But as I looked closer at the Bible, I began to discover the modernist bias that blinded me. I began to discover a different picture than the one I had painted myself into.

bezalel the artist

Philosophy and theology have traditionally been constructed from three components: metaphysics (reality), epistemology (knowledge) and ethics (morality). But I think another ancient formula (from Plato) gets it more right: the Good, the True and the Beautiful. Aesthetics (the study of beauty) is as necessary to our theology as truth and goodness. Yet all too often, it is relegated to a supplemental or optional elective in the curriculum of our faith.

God considers beauty to be an integral part of our relationship with him. The artist is no mere hobbyist but rather a tool in the hand of God for accomplishing that purpose. A closer look at Scripture about the making of the first tabernacle for the worship of God helped to illuminate this importance for me:

> Then Moses said to the sons of Israel, "See, the LORD has called by name Bezalel the son of Uri, the son of Hur, of the tribe of Judah. And He has filled him with the Spirit of God, in wisdom, in understanding and in knowledge and in all craftsmanship; to make designs for working in gold and in silver and in bronze, and in the cutting of stones for settings and in the carving of wood, so as to perform in every inventive work. He also has put in his heart to teach, both he and Oholiab, the son of Ahisamach, of the tribe of Dan. He has filled them with skill to perform every work of an engraver and of a designer and of

an embroiderer, in blue and in purple and in scarlet material, and in fine linen, and of a weaver, as performers of every work and makers of designs."

"Now Bezalel and Oholiab, and every skillful person in whom the LORD has put skill and understanding to know how to perform all the work in the construction of the sanctuary, shall perform in accordance with all that the LORD has commanded." Then Moses called Bezalel and Oholiab and every skillful person in whom the LORD had put skill, everyone whose heart stirred him, to come to the work to perform it. (Ex 35:30—36:2)

It is not insignificant that this is the very first passage in the Bible in which God fills a person with his Spirit; *and that person was an artist.* It was not mere skill that was required to build this beautiful edifice. It would take an artist to fulfill that blueprint from God. We're also told God filled Bezalel with wisdom, understanding, knowledge and artistic craftsmanship. The exact same traits God grants to

The Tabernacle

prophets (Num 24:16), priests (1 Sam 2:35), and kings (1 Kings 5:12), yet here he puts it all into an artist. And this wasn't an isolated incident. Later, another artist by the name of Hiram is described as being filled with "wisdom, understanding and skill" (1 Kings 7:14), and Huram-abi is yet another artisan called a "skilled man, endowed with

Solomon Builds the Temple, by Julius Schnorr von Carolsfeld

understanding" (2 Chron 2:13). Artists have a high calling from God.

The tabernacle (and by extension, later, the temple) was the heart of the Jewish religion, the very place of God's presence in their midst (2 Chron 5:13-6:2). It was the means through which they received atonement for sins. It was the symbolic center of the universe.[1] So God did

---

[1]As explained later in this book, when God establishes his covenant, he calls it "establishing the heavens and the earth" (Is 51:15-16), and when the temple, as emblem of that covenant, is destroyed in Jeremiah's time, it is described in terms

not take art lightly. But it is important to note here that God did not give every detail of the design, weaving, embroidery and engraving. God left many of the details to the artisans themselves. And he used an internal calling to draw the artists. Art was a holy calling to God, but it was a subjectively experienced one ("everyone whose heart stirred him").

Lastly, art is not merely a calling, but creativity is shown in Scripture to be a gift from God. The Lord is described as "putting skill" into the artisans and "filling them with skill." To God, art is not a mere personal fancy, or a side hobby to the real calling in life, like "preaching the Gospel" or some other "spiritualized" sacred thing. No, art is a spiritual calling just as much as prophet, priest or king.

So by way of summary, this passage points up several important aspects of the value of art and artists to God:

- God fills artists with his Spirit.

- God values art highly.

- God values artists highly.

- Art is a calling from God.

- Creativity is a gift of God.

signs and wonders

Roughly 30 percent of the Bible is rational propositional truth and laws, while 70 percent of the Bible is story, vision, symbol and narrative—that is, *image*.[2] The thousands of miracles that God performed

---

of the universe returning to the original "darkness and void" of Genesis 1:2 (Jer 4:23 -27).

[2]My actual research uncovered 20 percent propositional truth, 80 percent story, vision, symbol and narrative. But I added a handicap of 10 percent to the propositional side so I could not be accused of blinded prejudice. Of course, most of the propositional content and imagery is integrated with each other, so a strictly "scientific" separation is not possible. Both are necessary to God's revelation, but the sheer comparison of volume is illuminating.

for his people were not abstract propositions, but sensate visual signs (images) intended to elicit faith and trust in their Creator.

It is no coincidence that the phrase "signs and wonders" is used by biblical writers. A "sign" is a visual experiential symbol pointing to truth or proving a proposition (Heb 2:4).[3] So one of God's most dramatic means of persuasion recorded in the Bible is through the signs or *images* of miraculous wonders.[4]

The Healing of the Lame Man (Acts 3:1-8),
by Julius Schnorr von Carolsfeld

dreams and visions

And then there are dreams and visions—God's form of television

---

[3]See also Deut 6:22; Dan 4:1-3; Acts 14:3; 2 Cor 12:12.

[4]It is important to note that while God used miracles as signs or verification, he did not intend them to be absolute or ultimate in terms of proof. Faith is the biblical ultimate: Jn 4:48; Lk 16:31; 2 Cor 5:7.

and movies: Joseph's dreams of fat and skinny cows (Gen 41), Ezekiel's spinning wheels (Ezek 1) and valley of dry bones (Ezek 37), Nebuchadnezzar's nightmare statue (Dan 2), as well as other visions given to key figures throughout the Old Testament.

It doesn't end there. God uses visual images in dreams and visions to New Testament believers such as Ananias (Acts 9:10), Joseph (Mt 1:20), Peter (Acts 10:10-11) and Paul (2 Cor 12:1-4). The apostle Peter reiterates the significance of visions and dreams on the Day of Pentecost:

> This is what was spoken of through the prophet Joel: "And it shall be in the last days," God says, "That I will pour forth of My Spirit upon all mankind . . . And your young men shall see visions, And your old men shall dream dreams." (Acts 2:16-17)

The Prophet Daniel, by Julius Schnorr von Carolsfeld

No matter how one defines "last days" in this passage, the point remains: images are still an important means to God for communicating truth under the New Covenant.

the visual word of god

God does not consider imagery to be an inadequate or inferior means of communicating as compared with words. In fact, he often considers image to be equally important with words, or he wouldn't have used so much visual imagery described *as his word*. Which raises the question: Are dreams and visions, signs and wonders really all that different from words?

In Isaiah 2:1 we read about Isaiah's vision: "the *word* which Isaiah the son of Amoz *saw*."[5] In Micah 1:1: "the word of the Lord which came to Micah . . . which he *saw*." In Isaiah 13:1 and Habakkuk 1:1 the expression, "the oracle which the prophet *saw*" is used synonymously with God's "Word."[6] In Ezekiel 1:1-3, we read Ezekiel telling us that his visions of God are "the Word of the Lord." The prophet Zechariah says that the "Word of the Lord" came to him "as follows," and then he recounts the vision he *had* (Zech 1:7-8). Amos says of God's revelation to him in several places, "the Lord God *showed* me" (Amos 7:1, 4; 7, 8:1). When God pictures his "Word" to Amos, Zechariah and Jeremiah, he asks them, "What do you *see*?" (Amos 7:8; 8:2; Zech 4:2; 5:2; Jer 1:11, 13; 24:3). God did not float Hebrew words in the air like ancient sky-writing. He is defining image-based *visions* as his *Word*.[7]

Speaking of God's visual Word, the last book in the Bible—God's final word to us—is an epic vision, a feast of visual imagery and

---

[5]See also Isaiah 1:1 and 13:1 to the same effect.

[6]See also Nahum 1:1. The Hebrew for "oracle" means "utterance."

[7]One exception to this rule is Dan 5:5, where God's hand *does* in fact engage in writing judgment on a wall in Aramaic.

The Prophet Isaiah, by Julius Schnorr von Carolsfeld

theater. Regardless of one's interpretation of this mysterious book, the images of apocalyptic horsemen, multiple-headed beasts and monsters running around killing people in Revelation are more akin to a modern horror film or fantasy epic than a systematic theology or sermon.

As these passages illustrate, according to God's prophets, the very concept of "God's Word" is not an exclusively word-oriented concept. The visual imagery that God paints and dramatizes, just as much as anything he has verbalized through words, is God's *Word.* As theologian Kevin Vanhoozer points out, Scripture "is not merely the disclosure of information about God (revelation) but a collection of diverse kinds of divine communicative acts"[8]—images

[8]Kevin J. Vanhoozer, *The Drama of Doctrine: A Canonical-Linguistic Approach to Christian Theology* (Louisville, Ky.: Westminster John Knox, 2005), p. 47.

Detail of the Whore of Babylon, by Albrecht Dürer

and actions as well as literal *words* that are spoken or written. In fact, God's most important *word* is not a spoken or written word at all but an incarnate human being. Hebrews 1:1-2 proclaims that God, after speaking long ago through the prophets in many ways, has ultimately "spoken to us in His Son." We know about his Son through reading the words of Scripture, but what we know is not so much philosophical speculation about truth but dramatic incarnation of truth.

A common assumption among modernist Christians is that "preaching the Word of God" refers almost exclusively to a man standing on a podium elevated above an audience who are seated in pews all facing the speaker. This man lectures them for an hour or so as the climax of the "church service." Drama in such contexts is sometimes considered to be sacreligious. Many would not even begin to fathom the notion that art outside this church context could be a legitimate form of "preaching God's Word." Too bad for them, because God does.[9]

images of god

God does not merely use images to reveal his *message*. He often uses images to reveal *himself*. A burning bush (Ex 3:2), a pillar of cloud and a pillar of fire (Ex 13:21-22), a "glory cloud" that covered the tabernacle (Ex 40:34-35), and an angelic male messenger (Josh 6:12) are just a few choice examples. Consider the doz-

---

[9]It is important to note, of course, that God's visions, dreams, signs and wonders are almost always accompanied by (if not explained through) words. This should be a cautionary note to postmoderns who attempt to elevate image above word. But this mutual embeddedness of word and image does not suggest the superiority of either word or image, but rather their mutual dependency and equality of ultimacy in God's usage of language.

ens of metaphors used of God, such as a lion (Hos 5:14), a lamb (Rev 21:22), a shepherd (Ps 78:71), a farmer (Ps 80:8), a vinegrower (Is 15), a potter (Rom 9:20-23), even a drunken soldier (Ps 78:65), a father (2 Cor 6:18), a lover (Jer 3:20), a bridegroom (Is 62:5), a king (Ps 10:16), a consuming fire (Heb 12:29), a shield (Gen 15:1), a rock (Ps 18:46), a fortress (Ps 31:3), a cornerstone (Is 28:16), a morning star (Rev 22:16), a hen (Mt 23:37) and an eagle (Jer 49:22). Some of God's favorite images to use for his presence are thunder, lightning, clouds, smoke, and fire (Ex 19:16-18; Rev 11:19). Ezekiel's famous vision of God's glory included many-faced, many-winged, genetically spliced creatures around a throne with wild whirling wheels and a man of glowing metal and radiant fire in the center (Ezek 1)—one of the most interesting visuals in all the Bible, a stunning high-definition, Dolby sensurround feast.

The fact that God uses anthropomorphisms—human traits attributed to a nonhuman subject—to talk about himself is a powerful indicator of the value of imagination and human imagery in communicating and understanding truth. In the pages of the Bible, God is described dozens upon dozens of times as having eyes (Prov 15:3), ears (1 Pet 3:12), a nose (Gen 8:21), a face (Ps 114:7), arms (Ezek 20:33), and hands (Mk 12:36) with fingers (Deut 9:10), feet (Ex 24:10), a heart (Gen 6:6), a mouth (Is 1:20) with lips (Job 11:5) that even vomits (Rev 3:16). These are not physical descriptions; God is a spirit, not a physical body (Jn 4:24). These images, then, are obviously used as metaphors for us to understand God as personal, rather than abstract. Even though God uses reason and is referred to as the Logos (Jn 1:1), that Logos is biblically understood not as abstract rationality but as the *personal sustainer* of the universe, a spirit that became flesh (Jn 1:14), incarnate in the story of man. Word become image. But more on that a little later.

In addition to these cloaked images of God, the Scriptures also speak in dozens of places of God appearing without a description of how he appeared. Among these appearances God makes are to Abram (Gen 12:7), Isaac (Gen 26:2), Jacob (Gen 35:9), Amos (Amos 7:7), and Solomon (2 Chron 1:7). Speculation would be fruitless, but the point remains that appearances are visual or sensate experiences. In one instance, God is described as appearing through his spoken words alone (1 Sam 3:21), which once again illustrates the interconnectedness of words and imagery, but is certainly not the hermeneutical key to all the other appearances, since they involve the language of visual sight.

drama, theater and parable

Rather than merely give sermons, God often had his prophets give plays. Isaiah's shocking performance art was to walk around naked as a *visual* "sign and token" of the shame Israel was about to experience at the hands of Egypt (Is 20:2-4). Ezekiel could be considered a thespian prophet. God told him to perform a war epic as a prophecy, complete with a miniature city besieged by battering rams (Ezek 4:1-3). Then God has Ezekiel engage in the longest performance art prophecy ever recorded by laying on his sides for 430 days, tied up in ropes, eating food cooked over burning excrement, with an emblem of the sins of Israel on top of him (Ezek 4:4-8). He concludes this performance by cutting his hair and beard, and dispersing it in various ways to dramatically depict God's concluding judgment (Ezek 5:1-4). God then had Ezekiel perform a theatrical prophecy of exile by covering his face, dragging his baggage around day and night, and digging a hole in a wall to store it, all while saying "I am a sign to you" (Ezek 12:1-11). Ezekiel then had to tremble and shudder while eating as another dramatic sign of the anxiety that Israel will feel in their exile (Ezek 17—20). And later, God had him perform a sign of two sticks, symbolizing Judah and Israel, becoming one, not unlike a magician before his audience (Ezek 37:15-23). Mere words were not enough for God. He wanted spectacle; he wanted lights, camera, action!

The Prophet Ezekiel, by Julius Schnorr von Carolsfeld

Jeremiah is called "the weeping prophet." But he should have been called "the acting prophet," because so many of his prophecies were theatrical performances: hiding his girdle by the Euphrates (Jer 13:1-11), breaking a potter's bottle in the valley of Hinnom (Jer 19:1), walking through all the gates of Jerusalem (Jer 17:19-27), wearing a yoke on his neck (Jer 27:1-14), purchasing the deed to a field (Jer 32:6-15), burying stones in some pavement (Jer 43:8-13), and casting a scroll into the Euphrates (Jer 51:59-64).

The prophet Nathan tells a parable to King David in order to bypass his intellectual rationalization (2 Sam 12:1-7). Another prophet physically wounds himself to embody God's word to Ahab (1 Kings 20:35-43). God commands Hosea to marry the prostitute Gomer in order to dramatically and existentially personify Israel's spiritual adultery and God's grace (Hos 1:2; 3:1). And the children of Hosea become incarnational images of the New Covenant promise.[10] Even more dramatic and existential, God takes the life of the prophet Ezekiel's wife as a sign for how he will treat rebellious Israel during the captivity under Babylon (Ezek 24:15-27). In the New Testament, God uses the visual spectacle of a picnic blanket filled with unclean

The Prophet Jeremiah, by Julius Schnorr von Carolsfeld

---

[10]Hosea's first child is named Jezreel, which means "scattered by God," predicting the Diaspora of the Jews. The second child's name, Lo-Ruhamah, means "without mercy," and the third, Lo-Ammi, means "not my people." God then summarizes this incarnational prophecy of images in Hosea 1:10, which is quoted by Paul in Romans 9:25-26 as a prophecy of the New Covenant.

animals to persuade Peter of the New Covenant inclusion of Gentiles (Acts 10). Agabus binds his hands as a prophetic enactment of Paul's future in Rome (Acts 21:11).

Several books of the Bible are deliberately structured according to theatrical conventions. The books of Job and Jonah are depicted in dialogues reminiscent of ancient plays, including prologues, epilogues and several acts. Job's friends function as the chorus of ancient theatrical performances. God's theological discourse with Job is not so much a rational lecture of truth as it is a dramatic exhibition of sarcastic rebuke—all from within a sensational tornado as God's microphone. The book of Mark resembles a Greek tragedy following Aristotelian structure, involving a prologue (Mk 1:1-15), complications (Mk 1:16—8:26), a recognition scene (Mk 8:27-30) and a reversal of the fortunes of the leading character followed by the denouement (Mk 8:31—16:8).[11]

That Scripture follows conventional, even pagan art forms does not imply that Scripture is fictional. God considers theatrical expression to be a highly valuable means of communicating truth even if modern Christians do not. In fact, the use of narrative and drama to communicate God's Word and covenant is so prevalent in Scripture that some theologians suggest we approach our theology in dramatic terms rather than the usual modernist metaphysical terms of facts, ideas and propositions. Kevin Vanhoozer suggests we see the Bible not as "a handbook of revealed information, the systematization of which leads to a set of doctrinal truths," but as a dramatic script written by God for the stage of the world, with humans as the actors, God as the author, the Holy Spirit as director, and the church as playing out the final act. "To become a Christian is to be taken up into the drama of God's plan for creation."[12] Theol-

[11]"Theater," *Dictionary of Biblical Imagery*, OakTree Software.
[12]Vanhoozer, *Drama of Doctrine*, p. 71.

Job Laments His State, by Julius Schnorr von Carolsfeld

ogy is not an intellectual excercise of mentally constructing an accurate picture of reality in our ideas—and of "being right." It is a theatrical performance, where Christians participate in God's story of redemption. In this sense, our understanding of God is not so much *theology* (the study of God's Word), but *theo-drama* (the performance of God's Word).[13]

story conventions in the bible

Modernists tend to be suspicious of claims that Scripture follows conventional art forms because they assume this places an artificial constraint on the Word of God. "Straightforward" historical accounts or "eyewitness testimony" is considered to be the unadulterated presentation of God's truth. But all historical eyewitness

[13]Ibid.

accounting or telling of history follows cultural norms and structures, oftentimes even pagan ones. There is simply no such thing as a stripped-down "account of history" without human convention or interpretation.

For example, the covenantal structure that many scholars have discovered in biblical covenants as well as the literary structure of the entire Pentateuch reflects the structure of Ancient near Eastern pagan Suzerain treaties between conquering kings and their vassal subjects.[14] Those scholars do not consider such accommodation as syncretism (compromise with the world) but rather an adaptation of cultural norms of communication. In the same way, dramatic structure applied to biblical events does not necessarily mean history or truth is being abandoned or altered but rather that all human understanding of truth is organized and structured according to some paradigm of interpretation. There are no brute facts. All literature is an author's interpretation.

Baruch Writing Jeremiah's Prophecies, by Gustave Doré

The legal structure employed in some Old Testament literature does not consist of actual legal documents, but legal communication *embodied in narrative.* In the same way, New Testament theology in such letters as Romans follows a linear and rational structure, but as scholar James D. G. Dunn points out, "is still far removed from

---

[14]Meredith G. Kline, *The Structure of Biblical Authority* (Eugene, Ore.: Wipf and Stock, 1997).

a dogmatic or systematic treatise on theology."[15] Romans, like all New Testament epistles, is written to a specific church addressing specific historical problems with practical application of doctrinal truth. This is not to deny the value of systematics or legal protocol but merely to dethrone these approaches from their modernist exaltation as highest priorities in understanding God.

It would be most appropriate to describe Scripture as eclectic in its approach to communication and persuasion. In his Gospel, Luke sets about to corroborate eyewitness testimony and settle some factual disputes, written toward a mostly Gentile audience. Matthew seems to focus on Jewish readers, stressing Old Testament messianism. John's Gospel reads like a hybrid of Qumran apocalyptic and Hellenistic wisdom.[16] Leviticus may stress legal liturgical details, but Job is an epic sweeping play. Both major and minor prophets are often written as lawsuits to a judge, but unlike modern legal procedure, they are written poetically and allusively. In fact, many biblical prophecies are virtual film festivals of shocking images, metaphors and similes.

The modern Cartesian emphasis on clear and distinct ideas (systematic theology and rational propositional discourse) has a difficult time pinning down the prophets' ubiquitous use of ambiguous metaphors, parables and symbols. To this day, theologians cannot agree on their interpretations of several prophetic visions with absolute

---

[15]James D. G. Dunn, *The Theology of Paul the Apostle*, (Grand Rapids: Eerdmans, 1998), p. 25.

[16]I am not suggesting that the Gospel of John is Hellenistic or that it evolved from Hellenism—as the history of religions school wrongly argues. There is simply a stylistic identification with, or reflection of, the surrounding Greek culture. We use the cultural genres that we are embedded within to communicate our unique perspective. The Gospel of John is more basically Jewish, indicating that it is a Hebrew subversion of Hellenistic genre rather than a synthesis of it. See James H. Charlesworth, ed., *John and the Dead Sea Scrolls* (New York: Crossroad, 1991). More on subversion in chapters four and five.

certainty. From Daniel's puzzling monsters to Revelation's mysterious beasts, God's images may be doorways into truth, but they are not always analytically precise or understandably clear (2 Pet 3:16).

Sometimes revelatory images are explained clearly (Gen 41:25-32), sometimes they are not (see Ezek 1; Mt 13:10-11; and the book of Revelation). And sometimes they are explained and yet remain obscure (Dan 7). Christians have battled without final resolution for centuries over the meaning of Gog and Magog in Ezekiel 38—39. Commentators agree that the Millennium passage (Rev 20) is one of the most difficult in Scripture to interpret. Is the book of Revelation a symbolic allegory of the cyclical history of the church, as in amillennialism; an ancient description of a literal future, as in premillennialism; or historical symbolism of past history, as in postmillennialism? Yet all of these interpretations are considered legitimate orthodox Christian alternatives. One of them may be right, but all of them could be wrong. Why wasn't God more clear? If only God would have given us a systematic theological index!

Ezekiel's famous epic vision of measuring the temple takes a full four chapters of description (Ezek 40—43). Even though God tells Ezekiel to describe this temple to the people of Israel (43:10-11), scholars have pointed out that this cannot be a literal rebuilt temple because its measurements exceed the capacity of Jerusalem to house it.[17] The measurements, though apparently precise, do not match Solomon's temple nor the actual Temple built by the Jews afterward. We might speculate from the New Testament that this is a spiritual symbol of the rebuilt temple that the body of Christ has become (Eph 2:19-21; 1 Cor 3:16; 6:19; 2 Cor 6:16), but this is still speculation, because God did not give a clear word of explanation.

This is not to say that truth or Scripture is relative or that allu-

---

[17]Patrick Fairbairn, *The Visions of Ezekiel* (London: Wakeman Trust, 1851, reprint 2000) p. 433.

siveness of meaning is a sign of unimportance, but only that our reasoning should be humbled. So-called rational certainty is simply not applicable to the many puzzling mysteries of Scripture. Maybe, just maybe, God didn't want the "precision" of systematic theology or "certainty" of scientific analysis, since he often avoided those ways of communicating in favor of narrative, aesthetic or poetic imagination.

The fear of ambiguity and allusive meaning causes modernist Christians to interpret biblical parables as containing one theological meaning. They want the parables and stories to be mere illustrations of a doctrinal idea. But this misses the heart and intent of ancient storytelling. Scholar Kenneth E. Bailey, an expert on Middle Eastern New Testament studies, explains that

> a biblical story is not simply a "delivery system" for an idea. Rather, the story first creates a world and then invites the listener to live in that world, to take it on as part of who he or she is. . . . In reading and studying the Bible, ancient tales are not examined merely in order to extract a theological principle or ethical model.[18]

Theologian Kevin Vanhoozer agrees that doctrinal propositions are not "more basic" than the narrative and in fact fail to communicate what narrative can. He writes in his book *The Drama of Doctrine*, "Narratives make story-shaped points that cannot always be paraphrased in propositional statements without losing something in translation."[19] If you try to scientifically dissect the parable you will kill it, and if you discard the carcass once you have your doctrine, you have discarded the heart of God.

---

[18]Kenneth E. Bailey, *Jacob and the Prodigal: How Jesus Retold Israel's Story* (Downers Grove, Ill.: InterVarsity Press, 2003), p. 51.
[19]Vanhoozer, *Drama of Doctrine*, p. 50.

Bailey concludes that such stories and parables are means of understanding truth through existential inhabitation of the story. As we enter into the stories and see ourselves in them, we see truth in a way that mere logical or doctrinal discourse simply cannot evoke. But such imaginative inhabitation of stories becomes messy for the Christian who wants to have rational certainty. It makes God's truth a bit too ambiguous and subjective.

Rather than ignoring portions of God's word which do not meet the scientific analytic precision of modernity, we should chasten our rationality. Analytic precision and systematic reasoning are not God's preferred means of communication. Imagination through word pictures and story, with their existential embodiment and their rational imprecision and ambiguity, is God-ordained language after all.

metaphor

Jesus taught about the kingdom of God mostly through parables. And those parables communicated invisible reality in terms of visible, sensate and dramatic images and metaphors. To him, the kingdom of God was far too deep and rich a truth to entrust to rational abstract propositions. He chose pearls, dragnets, leaven, mustard seeds, virgins, children, slaves, hired workers, vineyards, and buried treasure over syllogisms, abstraction, systematics or dissertations. And his usage of such metaphors and images was not a primitive form of discourse, as if ancient Jews were not sophisticated enough to understand abstraction. In fact, at the time of the writing of the New Testament, Israel was educationally immersed in the Hellenistic culture that dominated the Middle East with its heavily abstract thinking. Jesus could do abstraction. He chose not to.

It would be more accurate to suggest the other way around, that indeed, stories and parables may be superior means of conveying theological truth than propositional logic or theological abstraction. As scholar N. T. Wright suggests, "It would be clearly quite wrong to see these stories as mere illustrations of truths that could in principle have been articulated in a purer, more abstract form."[20] He reminds us that theological terms like *monotheism* "are late constructs, convenient shorthands for sentences with verbs in them [narrative], and that sentences with verbs in them are the real stuff of theology, not mere childish expressions of a 'purer' abstract truth."[21] Wright concludes that storytelling is in fact the way theology was done in both Testaments:

> If Jesus or the evangelists tell stories, this does not mean that they are leaving history or theology out of the equation and doing something else, instead. . . . [If] this is how Israel's theology . . . found characteristic expression, we should not be surprised if Christian theology, at least in its early forms, turns out to be similar.[22]

Brad Young, who has written in depth on the Jewishness of Jesus' theology, reminds us that the Western view of theology as a discipline is more philosophical than Jesus' own Eastern culture within which he taught.

> As Christians, we study God and systematize belief. The Eastern mind tends to view God through the emotions of human personality and individual experience. God is viewed through the lens of metaphors and parables of real life which make the abstract concepts more concrete.[23]

---

[20]N. T. Wright, *The New Testament and the People of God* (Minneapolis: Fortress, 1992), p. 77.

[21]Ibid., p. 78.

[22]Ibid.

[23]Brad H. Young, *Jesus the Jewish Theologian* (Peabody, Mass.: Hendrickson, 1995), p. 272.

Our Western bias toward rational discourse can too easily blind us to the biblical power of story and word pictures to embody truth. Bailey writes about the tendency of Western culture with its stress on reason and logic to reduce biblical metaphors and parables to mere illustrations of concepts, as if word pictures or images were not essential but rather mere window dressing to the teaching of theological truth. "This," he says, "is a time honored way to 'do theology.'" But then he enlightens us,

> There is, however, another way to create and communicate meaning. It involves the use of word pictures, dramatic actions, metaphors and stories. This latter method of "doing theology" shines through the pages of Scripture. Dale Allison has written, "Meaning is like water: it is shaped by the container it fills." The biblical writers and reciters make extensive use of metaphors, parables and dramatic actions. Jesus does not say, "God's love is boundless," Instead, he tells the story of the prodigal son. He does not say, "Your benevolence must reach beyond your own kith and kin." Rather, he tells the story of the Good Samaritan.[24]

Bailey sees Jesus as "clearly a 'metaphorical theologian' whose primary style of creating meaning was the skillful use of metaphor, parable and dramatic action."[25] And this "word picture" theology means that stories are not mere carriers of doctrine, as if they can be discarded once the doctrine or "truth" is figured out. A parable does not contain a single truth or doctrine. It is a complex web of relationships and ambiguity interacting with the audience and their understanding and misunderstanding of God. Stories must be inhabited by the audience for the truth to be understood properly.

---

[24]Bailey, *Jacob and the Prodigal*, pp. 21-22.
[25]Ibid., p. 22.

They cannot be separated from the truth they embody.[26]

The parable of the prodigal son, for instance, is a complex network of metaphors for Jesus (the father), Gentiles and outcasts (the younger son), self-righteous Jews (the older son) and their relationships. Bailey contends that the parable is not even intended to express salvation of an individual as much as it is intended to be a retelling of the story of Jacob (and therefore, the story of Israel) with Jesus as the replacement of Israel, along with other challenges to people's view of God.[27]

It was certainly an enlightening moment in my own life when I came to realize my modernist prejudice in considering modern theological terms superior to biblical imagery and stories. Table 2 is an example of the kind of comparisons I had to make to reflect on my modernizing tendency.

C. S. Lewis pointed out that the technical term for God, "The transcendent Ground of Being," is simply not as rich or full of meaning as the scriptural metaphor "Our Father who art in heaven."[28] Of course, the creation of theological terms is not inherently wrong, and metaphors are not the only way in which Scripture communicates God's attributes. But we have to be careful that our theological shorthand will not overshadow or replace biblical longhand. The very theological words themselves reflect the modernist tendency to reduce truth to scientific terminology (every word having the suffix of "ology" or "ence"), which may ultimately depersonalize faith and cast theology as a "scientific" study rather than a holistic biblical relationship with God.

Scholar Peter J. Leithart goes so far as to say that theology as

[26]Ibid., pp. 51-52.
[27]Ibid.
[28]Kevin Vanhoozer, "The Semantics of Biblical Literature," in *Hermeneutics, Authority and Canon*, ed. D. A. Carson and John D. Woodbridge (Grand Rapids: Zondervan, 1986), p. 78.

**Table 2. Modern Theological Terms and
Corresponding Biblical Images**

Modern Theological Term	Biblical Image
Omnipotence	God has a strong right arm (Ps 89:13)
Omnipresence	If I make my bed in Sheol, you are there (Ps 139:8)
Omniscience	God counts the hairs on your head (Ps 139:9)
Transcendence	People are grasshoppers to God (Is 40:2)
Immanence	You have enclosed me behind and before (Ps 139:4)
Immutability	God will not wear out like clothes (Ps 102:26)
Asceity	I am the Alpha and Omega (Rev 22:13)
Providence	We are the clay, God is our potter (Is 64:8)

modern Christians understand it is *against* the biblical approach to truth, precisely because theology uses a professional language that is academic and obscure, "whereas the Bible talks about trees and stars, about donkeys and barren women, about kings and queens and carpenters."

> Theology tells us that God is eternal and unchangeable in His being, wisdom, power, holiness, justice, goodness and truth. The Bible tells us that God relents because He is God (Joel 2:13-14), that God is "shrewd with the shrewd" (Psa. 18:25-29), that he rejoices over us with shouting (Zeph. 3:14-20), and that He is an eternal whirlwind of triune communion and love. Theology is a "Victorian" enterprise, neoclassically bright and neat and clean, nothing out of place. Whereas the Bible talks about hair, blood, sweat, entrails, menstruation and genital emissions.[29]

---

[29]Peter Leithart, *Against Christianity* (Moscow, Id.: Canon Press, 2003), pp. 46-47.

Israel's theology was *told as stories*. The organizing principles of Jewish theology are characteristically expressed through narratives of creation, election, exodus, monarchy, exile and return.[30] So it was most appropriate when Jesus and the apostles proclaimed the New Covenant as the fulfillment of those stories—in stories and parables as well. Wright, a Pauline scholar, points out that even the apostle Paul's most "emphatically 'theological' statements and arguments are in fact expressions of the essentially Jewish story now redrawn around Jesus."[31] He points out that for the early Christians, disputes "were carried on not so much by appeal to fixed principles, or to Jewish scripture conceived as a rag-bag of proof-texts, but precisely by fresh retellings of the story which highlighted the points at issue . . . not a theory or a new ethic, not an abstract dogma or rote-learned teaching, but a particular story told and lived."[32]

It would not be an exaggeration to suppose that Jesus would probably be scolded by conservative evangelical theologues for not taking the kingdom of God more seriously, because he seemed to spend most of his time telling confusing stories rather than tightly organized three-point sermons. And even worse, Jesus would often avoid explaining those stories, preferring the "dangerous" ambiguity that modern evangelicals complain leads to an unclear "gospel presentation" or subjective interpretation (Mt 13:10-15). Jesus just wasn't precise enough by modern theological standards. Jesus just wasn't a modern evangelical.

the tabernacle and temple

Even a cursory look at the visual detail that God dictated to Moses for the tabernacle illustrates that imagery is valuable to God; he commands it as part of the holiest of activities—worship.

---

[30]Wright, *New Testament*, p. 215.
[31]Ibid., p. 79.
[32]Ibid., p. 456.

Part of the traditionalist Christian suspicion of imagery in worship comes from a misinterpretation of the Second Commandment prohibiting the worship of images.

You shall not make for yourself an idol, or any likeness of what is in heaven above or on the earth beneath or in the water under the earth. You shall not worship them or serve them; for I, the LORD your God, am a jealous God. (Ex 20:4-5)

Some Christians expand the command against worshiping images into a broader suspicion of *all* images, as if God himself is telling us to avoid imagery in worship because images are manipulative and dangerous, and lead to idolatry.

This is a shameful distortion of Scripture that creates an unbiblical Christian culture. "To use in worship" is not the same thing as "to worship." Five chapters after God tells the Israelites not to make likenesses of things in heaven or on earth to worship them, he commands the Israelites to make likenesses of things in heaven and on earth *to use in their worship of God!* God directs artists to make images of angels on the Ark of the Covenant (Ex 25:18). He has them craft almond trees and blossoms on the Holy Place instruments (Ex 25:31). He tells them to make pomegranates on the hems of the high priest (Ex 28:33), along with stones on his breastplate that function as symbolic references to the twelve tribes (Ex 28:25). Later, when God has Solomon build the

Altar, High Priest and Ark of the Covenant

temple, he adds even more visual images of things in heaven and on earth: huge statues of angels in the Most Holy Place, *the location of the very presence of God* (1 Kings 6:23-27); an altar imaged as a molten sea on the back of a dozen oxen with a rim like a lily flower (2 Chron 3—4); angels, palm trees and flowers carved and engraved all over the place (1 Kings 6:35); and multitudes of beautiful materials, precious metals, precious stones, rare woods, exotic colorful linens and other

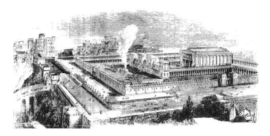

The Jerusalem Temple

architectural visuals (2 Chron 3—4). At the very heart of the covenant worship of God was *beautiful sensate imagery.*

To all this visual imagery, add loud music (1 Chron 23:5), hundreds of singers singing their theology through psalms (1 Chron 25:6-7) and myriads of dancers (Ps 150), and you have an image-rich experience of God. It now makes more sense what the psalmist meant when he wrote:

Molten sea laver

> One thing I have asked from the LORD, that I shall seek: That I may dwell in the house of the LORD all the days of my life, *To behold the beauty* of the LORD And to meditate in His temple. (Ps 27:4, emphasis added)

God's truth and beauty were reflected in the beautiful *imagery* of the temple. And the use of such manifold images in worshiping God was not inherently suspicious or idolatrous. Only the use of images as objects themselves of veneration would fit that category.

sacrament

Most Protestants agree that there are at least two sacraments in the Christian faith, Baptism and the Lord's Supper. Some theologians consider sacraments to be a "means" of grace. At the very least, they are visual *images* of our belief, or as Augustine put it, "the visible sign[s] of an invisible grace."[33]

Baptism is an experiential image of death to sin and resurrection in Christ (Rom 6:1-7), a cleansing of sin (1 Pet 3:18-21). The Lord's

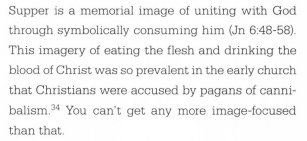

Supper is a memorial image of uniting with God through symbolically consuming him (Jn 6:48-58). This imagery of eating the flesh and drinking the blood of Christ was so prevalent in the early church that Christians were accused by pagans of cannibalism.[34] You can't get any more image-focused than that.

Such eating of the flesh of deity was also used by pagans (Jer 7:18), which leads some theologians to conclude that one evolved out of the other. But this evolutionary theory of the sacrament is a silly non-sequitur. Different religions use similar images because we all create from the same human pool of imagination and thought.[35]

---

[33]Allan D. Fitzgerald et al., ed., *Augustine Through the Ages* (Grand Rapids: Eerdmans, 1999), p. 707.

[34]From Minucius Felix, "Octavius," *The Ante-Nicene Fathers,* vol. 4, trans. R. E. Wallis, AGES Software (Albany, Ore.: AGES Software 2.0, 1997), pp. 348-49.

[35]The Aztecs, who ate sacramental bread as the flesh of a deity, had no cultural connection to the Middle East. From Sir James George Frazer, "Eating the God Among the Aztecs," in *The Golden Bough: A Study in Magic and Religion,* ac-

Most all modern evangelicals experience the Lord's Supper as a purely symbolic act in their church service. They eat a piece of bread or cracker and take a sip of grape juice or wine. But the first Christians had a fuller experience of the Lord's Supper as an embedded element of a total meal eaten together (1 Cor 11:20-23). The Lord's Supper was, after all, an adaptation of the Passover meal, also an entire meal eaten in its fullness as a sacramental experience, not a solitary symbolic gesture (Lk 22:7-20). In a way, evangelicals have wrested the symbolic act of communion from its more incarnate image of a full meal. *We have turned a meal that is symbolic into a symbol that is meal-like.* Why? Because word is more important to us than image. We tend to think that what's most important is the abstract idea, not the concrete experience, so why not reduce the idea of communion to its simplest symbolic act? And thus we build a version of Christianity that is more modernist than biblical.

Atonement through Christ's death on the cross was prefigured in Numbers 21, when God had Moses craft a bronze sculpture of a serpent on a pole to use as a sacrament of deliverance (healing) for those bitten by fiery serpents (Jn 3:14-15). We see from the episode that *visual art was used as a means of grace by God.* Later in 2 Kings 18:3-4, we learn that that image became an idol. But once again, we must note the difference between an image being used "in worship" as a sacramental means of grace and an image being an object of veneration or worship itself.

Those who argue for the priority of word over image will sometimes say that the images of sacraments are dependent on words for their meaning. Without textual context, for example, baptism remains mere splashing of water. Without verbalization of the meaning, the Lord's Supper is a mere meal. True enough. But this does

cessed February 5, 2008, at <http://www.bartleby.com/196/121.html>.

not prove the *superiority* of words over images but rather the *interdependency* of words and images. For without the incarnate experiences of splashing water and consuming the bread and wine, the

God Sends Fiery Serpents Among the People,
by Julius Schnorr von Carolsfeld

words remain mere abstractions. In sacrament, word and image are beautifully intertwined with equal ultimacy. You cannot have one without the other. The *Dictionary of Biblical Imagery* explains that

> the Bible is much more a book of images and motifs than of abstractions and propositions. . . . The stories, the parables, the sermons of the prophets, the reflections of the wise men, the pictures of the age to come, the interpretations of past events all tend to be expressed in images which arise out of

experience. They do not often arise out of abstract technical language. . . . The Bible is a book that images the truth as well as stating it in abstract propositions.[36]

The Bible is rich with images in its theological method and worship of God. It is filled with imagination and word pictures, overflowing with poetic language and sensate imagery, dominated by narrative or story. In contrast, modern theology's emphasis on systematic and scientific discourse places it in danger of not merely inadequacy but a serious misunderstanding of God, for the structure and method of theology affects the content of theology. If the Bible communicates God and truth (theology) primarily through story, image, symbol and metaphor, then a theology that neglects those methods is not being strictly biblical in its method. A scientific approach to God will ultimately depersonalize God through analysis and redefine Christianity through philosophical abstraction rather than embodying God's personal presence through lived-out stories.

So the question naturally arises, how did we get here? Where did this scientific and systematic suspicion and rejection of imagination start? That is for the next chapter.

---

[36]"Introduction," *Dictionary of Biblical Imagery*, OakTree Software.

FOUR

Iconoclasm

With all this imagery saturating the Scriptures, why is there such a lack of aesthetic understanding and development in the evangelical tradition? We find a partial answer in the iconoclasm of the sixteenth-century Reformation, which freed art from its captivity to the religious dogma of immanence but simultaneously recaptivated it to a new dogma of transcendence.

By the late Middle Ages (1300-1500), the Roman Catholic Church was the dominant religious force of the Western world. Its worship culture emphasized immanence—spiritual relationship with God was mediated through physical objects and the senses of the worshiper. This immanence stressed God's involvement with the created order, imparting grace or redemption through visible objects. Relics of alleged pieces of saints' bodies or fragments of Christ's cross were housed in shrines with altars, which the faithful would make pilgrimages to see. William Dyrness notes that these objects "not only reminded worshipers of supernatural reality but actually became a detached fragment of God's power."[1] Images of Christ and the saints, called "icons," became important theological tools for teaching the illiterate as well as objects of veneration.[2]

Liturgical drama—mystery plays, passion plays and miracle plays—was commonly used during this period to instruct peasants and celebrate feasts, festivals, and holy days. Churches were huge, glorious edifices full of wood and stone statues of the Virgin Mary, saints, prophets and martyrs; paintings of everything from the birth of Christ to his resurrection, and stained glass windows depicting the "stations of the cross." Medieval Christians of the era, Dyrness concludes, "took it for granted that the human relationship to God and the supernatural world was visually reflected and mediated through this visible order of things."[3] Scholar Margaret Miles explains that in an image-rich church,

> the worshipper was placed bodily in relation to a visually articulated spiritual universe. The present earthbound gravity of the individual worshipper was emphasized by his or her physical location beneath whirling scenes of heavenly bliss in which saintly human beings, angels, scriptural figures, and putti [winged cherubs] achieved a weightlessness that translated the ultimate goal of the spiritual life into visual terms.[4]

The Reformers saw such mediatorial art as distracting at best and idolatrous at worst. Ulrich Zwingli described the

---

[1]William A. Dyrness, *Visual Faith: Art, Theology and Worship in Dialogue* (Grand Rapids: Baker, 2001), p. 34.

[2]William A. Dyrness, *Reformed Theology and Visual Culture: The Protestant Imagination from Calvin to Edwards* (Cambridge: Cambridge University Press, 2004), p. 21.

[3]Ibid., p. 26.

[4]Margaret R. Miles, *Image as Insight: Visual Understanding in Western Christianity and Secular Culture* (Boston: Beacon Press, 1985), p. 110.

slavish devotion that parishioners would engage in before these images:

> Men kneel, bow, and remove their hats before them; candles and incense are burned before them; men name them after the saints whom they represent; men kiss them; men adorn them with gold and jewels; men designate them with the appellation merciful or gracious; men seek consolation merely from touching them, or even hope to acquire remission of their sins thereby.[5]

The cult of relics and images was vehemently preached against by the Reformers, and the people repented by vandalizing and destroying such images in churches throughout the land. Leaders of the Reformation condemned this vigilante iconoclasm as illegal and immoral, but they could not control the monster of vigilante iconoclasm they had birthed.[6]

THE ELEVATION OF THE WORD AND THE LIBERATION OF THE ARTS

Rather than being an *elimination* of visual culture, however, the iconoclasm *replaced* the visual culture of immanence with a visual culture of transcendence.[7] If immanence stressed God within the created order, transcendence stressed God's separation from the created order. Necessarily more abstract, transcendence became the new focus of Reformers such as John Calvin, who "privileged the ear over the eye" by elevating the written and preached word over the visual image as God's supe-

[5]Ulrich Zwingli, quoted in ibid., p. 99.
[6]Sergiusz Michalski, *The Reformation and the Visual Arts: The Protestant Image Question in Western and Eastern Europe* (New York: Routledge, 2005), p. 74.
[7]Dyrness, *Reformed Theology*, p. 6. See also, Margaret Miles, *Image as Insight*, pp. 122-23.

rior means of communication.[8] Margaret Miles describes it as a new "elitism of the word."[9]

The removal of images from churches gave visual expression to the belief that worshiping God was an internal spiritual matter, not an external one. Bare, stark white churches were not a rejection of imagery per se, but rather an attempt to refocus believers on the transcendent nature of God. Zwingli gleefully described churches in Zurich, Switzerland, "which are positively luminous; the walls are beautifully white."[10] This plainness of design lent a new voice to the role of minimalism and elegant simplicity in artistry, not to be confused necessarily with ugliness or lack of aesthetic.

Sola Scriptura, a key doctrine of the Reformation that Scripture alone was the final authority over the church, did not merely dismantle the hierarchy of power that the priesthood wielded over the masses. It also became an influence on the church architecture and worship as well.[11] As word became privileged over image, and the ear privileged over the eye, Protestant churches

---

[8]Dyrness, *Reformed Theology*, p. 6.

[9]Miles, *Image as Insight*, p. 104.

[10]Paul Corby Finney, ed., *Seeing Beyond the Word: Visual Arts and the Calvinist Tradition* (Grand Rapids: Eerdmans, 1999), p. 13.

[11]A corollary to this internalization of the truth from public concrete visual expression to personal inner abstract piety is the spectre of individualism. Author Daniel Hardy explains that Medieval churches "enacted communal society by extended liturgical performances," while Protestant meetinghouses, the replacement of Roman cathedrals, "housed the inner transformation of individuals by the preached Word of God" (quoted in ibid., p. 9.) The turn from externalized religion to internalized religion was not merely an exchange of outward idolatry with "true" spirituality as the Reformers claimed. It also tended toward an elevation of the individual conscience as supreme arbiter. Luther's famous stand of conviction, "my conscience is captive to the Word of God," is a profound break with the authoritarianism of the Roman Church and an expression of the Bible as supreme authority, but it also carried with it the seeds of individualism and sectarian dogmatism that led to intolerant splintering of Protestant creeds and churches, and in some ways, fueled the bloody Thirty Years' War (Kevin Vanhoozer, *Is There a Meaning in This Text?* [Grand Rapids: Zondervan, 1998], p. 171).

recentered the church service around the preached word.[12] All instruction, prayers and singing were organized around the preached word. Images on display were often typographic displays of Scripture; illuminated manuscripts, because their artistry supported the text of Scripture, continued to be created. Because of the Reformed belief in the priesthood of believers rather than a priesthood of elite religious authorities, all of life—not merely church life—became sacred. And that included the arts. Zwingli and Calvin never disparaged visual art used for "secular" purposes. Their focus was on images used in worship.[13] Consequently, the arts were liberated from a religious stranglehold of "grand ideological and religious systems."[14] In the words of William Tyndale,

> There is no work better than another to please God; to pour water, to wash dishes, to be a cobbler, or an apostle, all are one; to wash dishes and to preach are all one, as touching the deed, to please God.[15]

Martin Luther was even stronger in his denunciation of the secular-sacred dichotomy:

> The idea that the service to God should have only to do with a church altar, singing, reading, sacrifice, and the like is without doubt but the worst trick of the devil. . . . The whole world could abound with the services to the Lord, not only in churches but also in the home, kitchen, workshop, field.[16]

---

[12]Finney, *Seeing Beyond the Word*, pp. 8-9.
[13]John Calvin, *Commentary on Genesis*, vol. 1, Genesis 4:20 (Albany, Ore.: Ages Software 1.0, 1998); Michalski, *Reformation and the Visual Arts*, p. 71.
[14]Michalski, *Reformation and the Visual Arts*, p. 194.
[15]William Tyndale, *A Parable of the Wicked Mammon* (1527), accessed February 5, 2008, at <www.xristos.com/Pages/Quotes_page.htm>.
[16]Martin Luther, accessed February 5, 2008, at <www.xristos.com/Pages/Quotes_page.htm>.

One would not have to paint a scene from the Bible in order to honor God with their art. Simple ornamentation could do so. Still lifes took on a whole new sacred meaning, along with paintings of everyday life. Before this time, portrait painting was dominated by aristocracy and wealthy merchants. The Protestant Reformation brought a populist effect on aesthetics with an increase in art depicting the "common man."

The Calvinist concept of nature being God's "second book of truth" led to the origin and development of the famous seventeenth-century landscape art of the Dutch Netherlands.[17] Reformed artists like Albrecht Dürer are credited with being major influences on the origin of landscape painting, something that was considered without much merit until this paradigm change.[18] After all, if creation glorifies God as his handiwork of beauty, why wouldn't a simple landscape do so as well as an altar piece of the Last Supper?

The Enlightenment caricature of the Reformers as having a "horror of art" was a misrepresentation.[19] At the same time that Zwingli was removing pipe organs and images from the churches of Zurich, he was playing regularly in an instrumental group and illustrating his tracts on the Lord's Supper with wood engravings.[20] In a sense, Protestant iconoclasm made the whole of life religious, not merely church life, and it was the theological foundation of the liberation of the arts from exclusively ecclesiastical use. The Reformers were not opposed in principle to the

---

[17]Reindert L. Falkenburg, "Calvinism and the Emergence of Dutch Seventeenth-Century Landscape Art," in Finney, Seeing Beyond the Word, pp. 343-51.
[18]Gene Edward Veith, Painters of Faith: The Spiritual Landscape in Nineteenth-Century America (Washington, D.C.: Regnery, 2001), p. 21.
[19]Philip Benedict, "Calvinism as a Culture?" in Finney, Seeing Beyond the Word, p. 21.
[20]James R. Tanis, "Netherlandish Reformed Traditions in the Graphic Arts, 1550-1630," in Finney, Seeing Beyond the Word, p. 372.

arts, but rather to the adoration and sanctification of works of art in religious liturgy.

SUSPICION OF IMAGE AND DEVALUATION OF AESTHETICS

Yet, in spite of this artistic liberation that came through Reformation theology, evident in the music and art of the era (including Reformed masters such as Rembrandt and Dürer), there is nevertheless *a lack of visual and dramatic tradition* in Protestantism.[21] The Reformation suspicion of images soon bled into the prevailing secular culture to include many forms of imagination and creativity. As Dyrness notes, "all attempts at using imagery, drama, even cultural festivities, in the service of the communication of Christian truth appeared to be given up by around 1580."[22] It was a pendulum swing that would impact Protestant involvement in the arts for centuries to come.[23]

This extreme reaction is not entirely without justification, when one considers the tendency of human nature to be, as Calvin put it, a "factory of idols." In the same way an alcoholic abstains from drinking, so a populace infected with widespread idolatrous worship of images opted for a radical response. Martin Luther attempted a call to moderation, but such titans of the Word as Calvin, Zwingli, Knox, Bucer and others wrote extensively about the wrong use of images but comparatively little on the right use of the arts—occasional and scattered sidebars or tangents pertaining to a particular Scripture, but almost noth-

---

[21]Michalski, *The Reformation and the Visual Arts,* p. 40. See Veith's *Painters of Faith* for an excellent exploration of the Dutch tradition and its profound impact on landscape painting.

[22]Dyrness, *Reformed Theology,* p. 124. Also Benedict, "Calvinism as a Culture?" p. 31.

[23]Finney, *Seeing Beyond the Word,* p. 8.

ing of significant theological development.[24] The net effect of this virtual ignoring of the theological value of art is the implicit devaluing of it. As the saying goes, actions speak louder than words, and a systematic theology without a developed aesthetic is an implicit sign of an underlying belief that beauty is not an essential part of theology.

Calvin's prejudice was clearly didacticism, an elevation of utility and doctrinal teaching as the supreme form of communication. Thus, his tendency was to favor representational art of historical events used to "admonish" or "teach" over other imagery that was more decorative or abstract because they had "no value for teaching." In one of the only places where he writes more than a passing comment about art, Calvin refers to musical instruments, and by extension the other arts as well, as being able to "minister to our pleasure, rather than to our necessity, still it is not to be thought altogether superfluous; much less does it deserve, in itself, to be condemned."[25] Hey, at least it's not *altogether* superfluous; only *partially* superfluous.

In their appeal to divert the money for church decoration to the poor, Calvin and others unwittingly devalued art further.[26]

---

[24]Ibid., p. 79.

[25]"And yet I am not gripped by the superstition of thinking absolutely no images permissible. But because sculpture and painting are gifts of God, I seek a pure and legitimate use of each. Therefore it remains that only those things are to be sculptured or painted which the eyes are capable of seeing. . . . Within this class some are histories and events, some are images and forms of bodies without any depicting of past events. The former have some use in teaching or admonition; as for the latter, I do not see what they can afford other than pleasure. And yet it is clear that almost all the images that until now have stood in churches were of this sort. . . . I only say that even if the use of images contained nothing evil, it still has no value for teaching." John Calvin, *Institutes of the Christian Religion* 1:11:12 (Albany, Ore.: AGES Software 1.0, 1998).

[26]Michalski, *Reformation and the Visual Arts*, p. 69; and Benedict, "Calvinism as a Culture?" p. 28.

But both beauty and charity are important to God and both are necessary. God gave commands to love the poor (Deut 15) and collected massive amounts of money to build the splendorous Tabernacle (Ex 36), a model reflected in cathedrals and their ornamentation. Excess can be waste, but splendor and beauty are not intrinsically excess.

In Matthew 26, a woman pours expensive perfume on Jesus' feet. The disciples complain with a similar refrain to that of Luther and Calvin: "Why this waste? For this perfume might have been sold for a high price and the money given to the poor" (Mt 26:8-9). Jesus puts them in their place by saying that she has done a good thing, not a wasteful thing, in symbolic preparation for his burial. Perfume was used to mask the smell of death with an attractive aroma—a symbol of eternal life (Lk 23:56). Beauty is not waste. Christians, in their zeal for theology, often neglect the necessity for aesthetic beauty in their worldview.[27]

It could be said that the various Reformed strains of art that did survive the iconoclasm controversy did so in spite of the dominant voices of iconoclasts. Calvinists like Rembrandt would paint pictures of Christ despite the accusation by many that this was a violation of the Second Commandment. Calvinist Claes Jansz Visscher published Bibles heavily illustrated with engravings in an attempt to help people understand the stories better. (He also published political tracts against the iconoclasts.)[28] Albrecht Dürer, a Lutheran engraver, was praised by many Calvinists, despite his view that both eye and ear are necessary to our reality and relationship with God.

---

[27]See Calvin Seerveld, *Bearing Fresh Olive Leaves: Alternative Steps in Understanding Art* (Carlisle, U.K.: Piquant, 2000), pp. 1-5.

[28]Ilja M. Veldman, "Protestantism and the Arts: Sixteenth- and Seventeenth-Century Netherlands," in Finney, *Seeing Beyond the Word*, p. 417.

The art of painting is made for the eyes, for sight is the no-
blest sense. . . . A thing you behold is easier of belief than
[one] that you hear; but whatever is both heard and seen we
grasp more firmly and lay hold on more securely. I will
therefore continue the word with the work and thus I may
be the better understood.[29]

Dürer had it right. Both word and image were necessary. Perhaps what Calvin missed in his logocentrism was that the ear is
no more transcendent than the eye.[30] Both ear *and* eye are a
God-ordained sensate part of how we interact with him.[31]

DUALISM AND DICHOTOMY

The false separation of the senses leads to a matter-spirit dualism
in some Reformed theology that reflects the very secular-sacred
dichotomy that Reformers debunked.[32] Reformers claimed, for
example, that the immanent sensate worship of the Old Covenant
was surpassed by a transcendent "spirit" (read: "abstract") worship of the New Testament. Hebrews 9, for example, describes the
visual elements in the temple as but shadows of the true Tabernacle in heaven. The "spiritual" New Covenant is the fulfillment
of the symbolic imagery of the Old Covenant temple (considered
childish or immature); therefore, images are no longer important
to God in worship.[33] But this is surely a confusion of categories.

---

[29]Albrecht Dürer, as quoted in Margaret R. Miles, *Image as Insight,* p. 116.
[30]Dyrness, *Reformed Theology,* p. 69.
[31]Ibid., p. 121.
[32]While Luther was just as emphatic of God's transcendence, he did not embrace
the matter-spirit dualism of the others, seemingly maintaining an equal emphasis
on God's immanence in his theology. Consequently, Luther displayed "greater attention to buildings, liturgy and music as allies in Christian faith." Finney, *Seeing
Beyond the Word,* pp. 16, 28.
[33]"It is absurd to drag [temple imagery] in as an example to serve our own age. For
that childish age, so to speak, for which rudiments of this sort were intended is

It is not that the *visual imagery* of the temple is being superseded by an invisible abstraction. It is rather a *temporary incarnation* being replaced with an *eternal incarnation*. Hebrews 10:1 says the Old Covenant law and temple are only shadows of the heavenly temple. But that heavenly temple is no less sensate. When we are resurrected, we will be so in our physical bodies, not abstract ones (1 Cor 15:12-56)—imperishable and transformed bodies, but physical ones with senses, just like Jesus (1 Jn 3:2). So the "heavenly/shadow" comparison in this passage is not one of sensate versus abstract but perishable versus imperishable, temporary versus eternal.

When Jesus told the Samaritan woman that people would no longer worship in this mountain or that, but that "true worshippers would worship the Father in spirit and in truth" (Jn 4:24), he was not discrediting Old Testament *imagery* in worship, he was discrediting localized cultural exclusion of other nationalities. Elsewhere in Scripture, we are told that the church is the body of Christ, which is the rebuilt temple that God promised (Acts 15:13-18; Eph 2:19-22).[34] This is not the replacement of a physical image with an abstract spiritual idea but the *expansion* of the visible incarnation (image) of God's dwelling place from a specific geographical location to a worldwide universal location.

Both brick and mortar temple (Old Testament) and flesh and blood church (New Testament) are physical tabernacles of God (2 Cor 6:16). Neither is an abstract thought or spirit. In fact, the very atonement of Christ, since it is expressed in terms of Old Testament temple worship, cannot be understood in propositional abstractions apart from that imagery. The imagery has

---

gone by." Calvin, *Institutes of the Christian Religion* 1:11:3.
[34]See also 1 Cor 3:16; 6:19; Heb 12:18-22; 2 Cor 6:16.

not been *negated* but *fulfilled and extended* in its meaning. Old Testament imagery is the foundation for understanding the New Covenant, and as such, is still necessary to it.

In the mind of the Reformers, with their emphasis on transcendence over immanence, "the finite cannot contain the infinite."[35] While this slogan may be true of the works of human hands, what is the incarnation of Christ but finite humanity containing the infinite God? In the incarnation, the ontological and theological reality of transcendence and immanence coexist in harmony. More will be said on the incarnation in the next chapter, but suffice it to say that its balance of two opposites, as with any mystery doctrine (see table 3), is degraded by an emphasis of one extreme against the other.

The Bible affirms both the transcendence *and* immanence of God as equally ultimate, many times in the very same passage. For instance, Paul, when preaching to the pagans on Mars Hill, at the same time affirms God's transcendence ("God does not dwell in temples made with hands") and immanence ("in Him we live and move and exist," Acts 17:24, 28). Jeremiah 23:23 asks rhetorically, "Am I a God who is near [immanence], declares the LORD, and not a God far off [transcendence]?" Colossians 1:16-17 says that all things were created "by him, through him, for him" (transcendence) "and in him all things hold together" (immanence). So a theology that fails to affirm God's transcendence and immanence with equal ultimacy is not true to the Scriptures, even if it is true to the *Institutes of the Christian Faith.*

---

[35]Carlos M. Eire, *War Against the Idols: The Reformation of Worship from Erasmus to Calvin* (Cambridge: Cambridge University Press, 1986, 1998), p. 2. Also Finney, *Seeing Beyond the Word*, p. 4.

**Table 3. Mystery Doctrines of the Bible, and the Distortions
That Accompany Dualistic Separations**

One —————————	**TRINITY** —————————	**Many**
Unitarianism	(John 1:1)	*Tritheism*

God —————————	**CHRIST** —————————	**Man**
Docetism	(John 1:14)	*Arianism*

God's Sovereignty ————	**PROVIDENCE** —	**Human Responsibility**
Fatalism	(Isaiah 10:12-15)	*Pelagianism*

Word —————————	**TRUTH** —————————	**Image**
Modernism	(John 1:14)	*Postmodernism*

Law —————————	**GOSPEL** —————————	**Grace**
Legalism	(Romans 3:20-24)	*Antinomianism*

Transcendent —————	**GOD** —————	**Immanent**
Existentialism		*Pantheism*
Deism	(Acts 17:24, 28)	

FIVE

INCARNATION

In 2004 the movie *The Passion of the Christ* was released to an American box office bonanza of over $400 million. Evangelicals and unbelievers alike filled the theaters for this image-rich, experiential interpretation of the Gospel narratives, connecting to it in more numbers than any other filmic presentation of Christ.

Evangelicals could never have made this movie. Roman Catholic Mel Gibson was barraged with "suggestions" by well-meaning evangelical screeners of the movie to place Bible verses such as John 3:16 ("For God so loved the world that He gave His only Son") at the end because they felt that it wasn't a clear enough presentation of the gospel. If it does not have words, then it is not a reliable or trustworthy communication to moderns.

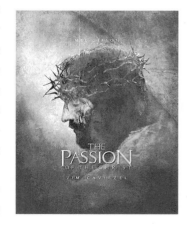

The movie *did* have words, plenty of them, and even a Bible verse to set

Christ Bearing the Cross,
by Albrecht Dürer

the stage for the meaning of the violent experience the viewer was to be immersed within. It just wasn't John 3:16. It was instead Isaiah 53:5: "He was wounded for our transgressions, crushed for our iniquities; by his wounds we are healed."

Ironically, given that evangelicals have regularly boycotted R-rated movies because of sex and violence, *The Passion* is arguably one of the most violent mainstream films ever made.[1] It took a Tridentine Roman Catholic to translate the Gospels to a postmodern, image-oriented culture, because Roman Catholics maintain a theology of immanence that Protestants have overshadowed with a theology of transcendence.[2]

IMMANENCE AND IDOLATRY

Some Evangelicals and Reformed believers read the Second Commandment—which forbids graven images of God—and conclude that pictures or movies of Jesus Christ are inherently idolatrous. This kind of reasoning led to the exclusion of the *Jesus Film Project* from a recent convention of a major Reformed denomination. *The Jesus Film* is a movie of Jesus' life and ministry strictly adapted from the Gospel of Luke. According to Project statistics, six billion people in twenty-nine years—more people than any ministry in the entire history of Christianity—have been exposed to the gospel through the narrative and moving images of this film.[3] Yet it wasn't acknowledged as a legitimate ministry of the gospel by at least one Christian denomination.

---

[1]The claim that it is appropriate violence because it is in the context of redemption and faith simply points up the double standard that evangelicals hold in their rejection of other violent or profane movies that are equally redemptive in their context. I write more about this in *Hollywood Worldviews: Watching Films with Wisdom and Discernment,* updated ed. (Downers Grove, Ill.: InterVarsity Press, 2009).

[2]It is no coincidence that Gibson's production company is called Icon Entertainment. Icons are images of veneration dating back to medieval Christianity.

[3]Accessed February 5, 2008, at <http://www.jesusfilm.org/progress/statistics .html>.

Theologian Ken Gentry writes of the danger of confusing categories when addressing the prohibitions of images as a prohibition of Jesus Christ's human form:

> A picture of Christ is a picture of his humanity, for he does, in fact, possess a truly human body (as well as a truly human soul). A picture of Christ is not a picture of his inner, divine essence, nor even of his soul. Rather it is a picture of his external bodily form. Thus, a picture of Christ's human form is a picture of his humanity, not his deity; it is a picture of man (the God-man), not a picture of God.[4]

Of course, how one pictures Jesus also reflects one's theology, and that theology could itself be unbiblical. For instance portraying Jesus as a spiritual being whose speaking is always underlined by angels singing could reflect a Gnostic interpretation of Jesus as lacking in flesh and blood humanity. But likewise, the desire to stress Jesus' human side can become equally aberrant in separating him from his deity.

The superiority of Christ over previous revelation lies in his *incarnation*—his becoming flesh, a physical manifestation in time and space, beyond mere abstraction. Notice the opening words of the book of Hebrews:

> God, after He spoke long ago to the fathers in the prophets in many portions and in many ways, in these last days has spoken to us in His Son. . . . And He is the radiance of His glory and the exact representation of His nature. (Heb 1:1-3)

---

[4]Ken Gentry, "Christ, Art, and the Second Commandment," position paper by the author. Available at www.kennethgentry.com.

The incarnation is here intentionally spoken of in terms of a *visualization* of God's glory. The Greek word used for "exact representation" is *charaktēr,* which was a tool for engraving.[5] Remember the Second Commandment? "Thou shalt not make unto thee any graven image" (KJV). Jesus is referred to in terms of the very thing God prohibited to us: graven imagery.

This theme is reiterated in Colossians 1:15 where Jesus is referred to as "the image of the invisible God." The word for image there is *eikōn,* from which we get the English word, "icon," a statue or likeness.[6] In the ancient world, a king would represent his dominion in provinces where he could not personally  appear with the erection of images *(eikōns)* of himself.[7] Jesus Christ is God's personal *eikōn,* the visible representation of God's presence in time/space history.

This is not to say that God the Father or God the Spirit are physical and have a beard and look like the man Jesus. And it does not mean that God can be worshiped through pictures, sculptures or other visual images. But it also cannot mean merely that Christ reflects God's character in his behavior alone. Paul is using a visual metaphor for a reason. The theological concept of incarnation involves living embodiment, the visible expression within time and space of what is otherwise unseen. As the apostle John writes, "The Word became flesh, and dwelt among us, and we saw His glory, glory as of the only begotten from the Father, full of grace and truth" (Jn 1:14).

John emphasizes the image aspect of the incarnation not merely in

---

[5]*Strong's Greek Dictionary of the New Testament* 2.2 (Oaktree Software).
[6]Ibid.
[7]Gerhard von Rad, "εἰκών," in *Theological Dictionary of the New Testament,* ed. Gerhard Kittel, trans. Geoffrey W. Bromiley, 4 vols. (Grand Rapids: Eerdmans, 1964), 2:392.

"beholding his glory," but also in the phrase "dwelt among us," which is a translation of the Greek word for "tabernacle," or "pitching his tent."[8] Jesus is the New Testament *image* of the tabernacle of God's presence. Even if this were merely a reference to Christ's behavior, it would be experiential reality in concrete history, not philosophical speculation of abstract virtues.

Jesus as the incarnate Word is not a self-evident axiom or timeless principle of reason. He is not reducible to propositional syllogisms. At the heart of Christianity is not merely a philosophy or worldview but an incarnate person. Christian theology should maintain an equal ultimacy of both word *and* image because at the core of our faith is this equal ultimacy in the incarnation: Word made flesh.

INCARNATION, STORY AND PERSUASION

Images are concrete expressions of abstract ideas, the existential embodiment of the rational word. Images, whether they are stories, pictures or music, are *incarnations* of ideas—words made flesh. Image is the personification of logic, the enfleshment of proposition. C. S. Lewis valued myth because in it "we come nearest to experiencing as a concrete what can otherwise be understood only as an abstraction. . . . It is only while receiving the myth as a story that you experience the principle concretely."[9] Theologians Gordon Fee and Douglas Stuart admit that the narrative nature of biblical revelation allows us "vicariously to live through events and experiences rather than simply learning *about* the issues involved in those events and experiences," because "the Bible is not a series of propositions and imperatives; it is not simply a collection of 'Sayings from Chairman God' as though he looked down at us from heaven and said, 'Hey you down there, learn

---

[8]*Strong's Greek Dictionary of the New Testament.*
[9]C. S. Lewis, *God in the Dock: Essays on Theology and Ethics,* ed. Walter Hooper (Grand Rapids: Eerdmans, 1970), p. 66.

these truths.'"[10] Narrative imagery incarnates truth.

Incarnation is one of the most powerful means of communication. Whether we relate to a character in a story, enter the world of a painting, feel the heart of a song or embrace the joy of a dance, we are making a connection with truth or ideas through existential experience of what is otherwise an abstract proposition. People are rational beings, but more so, we are *personal* beings. We are incarnate.

Movies are one of the modern world's strongest examples of storytelling. When you watch a movie, you are watching a story that is an incarnation of a worldview. The hero embodies the superior worldview; the villain, the inferior worldview. The drama of the story comes from the conflict of their opposing worldviews, which drive their actions to conflict with each other. By the end of the story, the hero's worldview is proven superior to the villain's in his victory over the villain. Robert McKee sees story as

> humanity's prime source of inspiration, as it seeks to order chaos and gain insight into life. Our appetite for story is a reflection of the profound human need to grasp the patterns of living, not merely as an intellectual exercise, but within a very personal, emotional experience. In the words of playwright Jean Anouilh, "fiction gives life its form."[11]

Story incarnates the abstract concept of dialectical argumentation: thesis, antithesis, synthesis. And it is through incarnation, through the embodiment of worldviews and their resultant human behavior that story connects so deeply with the human psyche. As we identify or sympathize with the hero, we enter into his worldview, and experience the dialectic with him.

---

[10]Gordon Fee and Douglas Stuart, quoted in Kevin J. Vanhoozer, "The Semantics of Biblical Literature," in *Hermeneutics, Authority and Canon*, ed. D. A. Carson and John D. Woodbridge (Grand Rapids: Zondervan, 1986), pp. 80-81.
[11]Robert McKee, *Story: Substance, Structure, Style and the Principles of Screenwriting* (New York: HarperCollins, 1997), p. 12.

A good example of the power of image to embody otherwise rational argumentation is the movie *The Exorcism of Emily Rose*. Writer and director Scott Derrickson tells the story of a Roman Catholic priest on

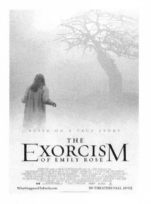

trial for criminal negligence in the death of a college girl named Emily Rose. Emily had come to the priest because she believed she was demon-possessed. In the midst of a laborious exorcism ritual, she died from self-inflicted wounds.

The protagonist of the story is Erin Bruner, a spiritual agnostic who serves as the priest's defense attorney. Throughout the trial the prosecutor mocks her attempt to prove the *possibility* of demon possession. Such superstitious arguments, he argues, are unbecoming of legal procedure in a modern scientific world. Emily had epilepsy, he attempts to prove, which required medication, not "voodoo."

The movie presents both sides of the argument so equally that the story leaves Bruner still an agnostic. But the viewer is left with a strong openness toward the legitimacy of a spiritual world, having been shown the raw experience of demon possession in contrast to the rationalizing tendency of scientism. Derrickson uses the story as a metaphor for the stranglehold of modernity on the western mind, and the inadequacy of rationalism and the scientific method in discovering all truth.

Story is persuasive because it embodies worldview in a narrative. In the same way that logic may follow a rhetorical structure, so story—and really all art forms—follows a structure that leads the audience to a conclusion. Most traditional stories as well as mainstream movies trace the redemption of the protagonist (or "hero"), a process used similarly by the apostle Paul in his testimony before King Agrippa (Acts 26). Figure 5.1 is the summary of this outline.

1. *Goal:* What the hero wants
2. *Plan:* How the hero will get what he wants
3. *Adversary:* Keeps the hero from getting what he wants (external)
4. *Flaw:* Keeps the hero from getting what he wants (internal)
5. *Apparent Defeat:* Circumstance that suggests the hero will not get what he wants
6. *Self-revelation:* Realization of the hero's flaw (internal)
7. *Final Confrontation:* Face-off between the hero and the adversary
8. *Resolution:* The change to the hero reflected in his life
9. *Theme:* What the hero learns through his story

Figure 5.1. Traditional rhetorical structure of a story. For a detailed explanation see Brian Godawa, *Hollywood Worldviews* (Downers Grove, Ill.: InterVarsity Press, 2009), pp. 79-86.

A story's hero seeks out his goal. An adversary seeks to stop the hero, but the hero is also confronted by an internal flaw. The obstacles in the story build to the point where it appears that the hero will never get what he wants. At the end of his rope, the hero has some kind of revelation about himself and his internal flaw—what he really wants is not what he really needs. By confronting that internal flaw, the hero finds what he needs to overcome his adversary and achieve what he really needs, and oftentimes also achieves what he originally wanted as well.

The drama of a story is the clash of worldviews, with one worldview—which the storyteller wants us to consider superior—arising as victor. Some protagonists, of course, don't change; these become the catalyst for others around him to change. In *Braveheart*, William Wallace is resolute in his determination to fight the king of England to the death for Scotland's freedom. Despite his death, his unyielding conviction becomes an inspiration to Robert the Bruce, who rises up to take Wallace's place.

But most protagonists emerge from their story changed. The character arc—the hero's journey from beginning through middle and on to the end—reflects the change in the hero's worldview. At the beginning of the story, there is a flaw in the hero's perception of the way things should be. As a result of his journey through the story, and because of the obstacles he faces, the hero learns something about the world that he did not know. That change of mind is the redemption of the hero.

Adversaries are not always evil villains in the traditional sense. Rather they serve to confront the hero's worldview and sometimes reveal the change necessary to the hero. In *Bruce Almighty,* Bruce is not satisfied with his life's circumstances. He thinks he can do better than God, so God gives Bruce his powers to teach him a lesson. Bruce discovers that he is not capable of "playing God," and he relinquishes his will back to God. Bruce's character arc goes from selfish and arrogant to selfless and humble before God. In this story, God is the adversary, but he turns out not to be a villain. Rather, God is the source of Bruce's learned wisdom.

IDENTIFICATION

Rather than making strictly logical arguments about truth or reality, a story carries us along existentially in a universe where arguments are incarnate, where worldviews are lived out and lead to positive or negative results. If the audience likes the protagonist, if they identify with him in some way, then they follow him on his journey and learn the lesson he learns along with him. This is why it is so important for the audience to be discerning about who they are rooting for. They are not merely being entertained when watching a movie or television show; they are being exposed to an incarnate argument about the way life ought or ought not be lived, about the nature of truth in human experience.

There are many ways that stories create a connection between the audience and the protagonist in order to persuade through identification. One is through sympathy; many people love to root for the underdog or the hero who has suffered great injustice. Humor is another basic way to draw the audience into the protagonist's viewpoint; audiences love to laugh at and with a humorous personality. Likeability is also a means of identification. People will like a protagonist even if he is a criminal, if that protagonist is perceived as cool.

Yet another means of identification with the audience is universal desire. If the hero is seeking something that we all seek in one way or another, then we relate to him and sympathize with him. Freedom, significance, protection of family, success, justice and love are all examples of universal desires that most of us can relate to.

LOVE INTEREST

The love interest in a story usually embodies what is lacking in the protagonist, the perfect complement to the hero. In order to discover his flaw, the hero has to lose his love interest. This is why the standard formula for love stories is (1) boy meets girl, (2) boy loses girl, (3) boy gets girl. Only by confronting his flaw and becoming a better person is the hero worthy of his lover. That is redemption.

REFLECTION

Another aspect of storytelling rhetoric is the reflection character, the person in the story who is going through the same problems but who seeks resolution in a different way. This is the dramatic way of discrediting counterarguments (antithesis) against the theme (thesis) of the story. In *Braveheart*, Robert the Bruce wants the same thing as William Wallace: a free Scotland. But he pursues this goal through negotiations and compromise with the king of England, rather than the uncompromising fight that Wallace engages in.

Bruce is the man of self-preservation and Wallace is the man of self-sacrifice. By seeing that the negotiation with the tyrannical king leads only to more slavery, the argument against compromise is sealed.

INCARNATION

Just as logical argumentation contains rhetorical rules of argumentation, so storytelling contains persuasive rhetoric. Let's take a look at just a few of the many other ways in which storytelling in movies uses the language of image and drama to effectively persuade the audience.

It is no surprise that stories that incarnate an idea can often have as much if not more impact than the labyrinthine meanderings of logical debate. Human beings are not reducible to disembodied intellects. We are also emotional beings whose reality is historically experienced within space and time. Truth is not merely mathematically measured against abstract doctrinal propositions; it is existentially experienced.

This goes for our approach to understanding the Bible as well. As Curtis Freeman puts it, we must read the Bible "not as disembodied minds seeking knowledge, but as embodied selves with histories searching for the story of our lives."[12]

---

[12]Curtis Freeman, "Toward a *Sensus Fidelium* for an Evangelical Church," in *The Nature of Confession: Evangelicals and Postliberals in Conversation*, ed. Timothy R. Phillips and Dennis L. Okholm (Downers Grove, Ill.: InterVarsity Press, 1996), pp. 164-65.

God used incarnation to communicate the seriousness of Israel's apostasy by commanding Hosea to marry the prostitute Gomer. The parable of the Good Samaritan is an incarnation of the argument defining the responsibility of loving one's neighbor as universally applicable to everyone, as opposed to the logical and legal technicalities used by the Pharisees to justify their lack of compassion.

SUBVERSION

Subversion—the retelling of one mythology in terms of another—is another rhetorical strategy of storytelling. The film *Underworld* uses the accepted mythologies of *Romeo and Juliet* and the horror genre of vampires and werewolves to address the controversial idea of interracial romance. The tribal families of vampires and werewolves have been feuding for centuries, killing each other in the dark of night. Along comes a hybrid vampire/werewolf that threatens the werewolves' sense of identity and the vampire's power over the werewolves. The hybridization of these two cultures threatens the power of the majority and the survival of the minority. Utilizing these other mythologies bypasses the deep-seated prejudices of viewers to address the thorny issue of racism.

The Scriptures are themselves acts of subversion. The apostle John subverts the Hellenistic doctrine of *Logos* in John 1:1, taking a term loaded with pantheistic worship of abstract Reason as the underlying order of the universe, and subverting it by redefining it as "becoming flesh" in the person of Jesus Christ.

ANALOGY

An analogy is an inference that if two things are similar in some ways, they are similar in other ways as well. Some Christian philosophers argue that all truth is analogous. That is, nothing can be known apart from comparing it to something already known or assumed.

In movies, images that embody a similarity between ideas connects those ideas in identity. For example, the movie *The Island* is a futuristic sci-fi story about a corporation that creates clones to harvest body parts for clients as needed. The clones are kept in isolation and in ignorance of their true identity. The corporation uses euphemisms of the clones—"products"—to dehumanize them. The corporation tries to kill the clones before they are discovered. Henchmen make their way through a series of clones suspended in large plastic bags; they look like fetuses in amniotic sacks. These clones are injected with drugs and the plastic sacks are slashed open. Others are put into a chamber to be gassed. A black man challenges the owner of the corporation, suggesting that this is how slaves were treated in early American history. Through all these analogous images, viewers are reminded of abortion, euthanasia, the Jewish holocaust and black slavery.

The evil of the Beast in the biblical book of Revelation is analogized in his many-headed, blaspheming and animalistic, flesh-eating nature, while the sacrificial and peaceful nature of the Lamb depicts Christ's purity and goodness. Nathan's parable to King David analogizes his murder of Uriah to a man stealing another man's only ewe lamb (2 Sam 12:1-7).

GENERALIZATION

In debate, generalization is usually considered a logical fallacy because it takes a particular example of something and generalizes to a universal, when in fact, this is not always true. This is also the problem of most prejudice in our culture. However, as the old adage goes, stereotypes exist because they are to some degree true. There is a sociological preponderance of certain character traits or behaviors in certain cultures.

The fact that not everyone of a cultural community is exactly the same does not disprove that there are in fact many who are. We are sociological creatures and as such display common traits in our communities. Many Christians in the evangelical culture use similar language that others do not, such as "born again," "saved," "the blood of Jesus." And so they also behave in similar ways such as "witnessing" or quoting the Bible. Animal rights activists, Wall Street financiers, Democrats, Republicans, soccer moms and Hollywood celebrities all have similar behaviors within their cultural communities.

In a story, placing common phrases into a character's mouth or common behaviors in their actions identifies them with a certain cultural community. The character becomes a symbol for that community. The more common phrases and behaviors displayed in the character, the more easily universalized they are. And when the storytellers make those linguistic and behavioral connections, and then show the consequences on that character, they are incarnating the argument against that worldview.

The villain in *The Island* is the head of the corporation. He explains his motivations using the familiar language of modern scientists: the clones have no souls; they are a means to good ends for society, such as the curing of diseases like Leukemia. Modern scientists make similar arguments to justify public funding or approval of controversial schemes, such as embryonic stem cell research. By placing that familiar language in the villain's mouth, the storyteller makes a general connection of those ideas with villainy. This may not seem fair or logical to those who disagree, but it is the nature of storytelling to embody a worldview or paradigm in its characters.

Jesus' parables contain many examples of generalizations of different kinds of people. The snooty self-righteous religious hypocrite was one of his favorites (Lk 10:25-37; 18:10-14; Mt 23).

SYMBOLISM

In a story, a character may become a symbol for a particular worldview; the consequences of that character's experience become a symbol for what that worldview leads to. In *A Beautiful Mind*, the schizophrenic John Nash is a symbol for modernity: reducing truth to mental reasoning cripples our humanity, just as Nash was crippled by his

"disease." As a doctor tells Nash, his mind is his problem. He can't reason his way out. And by the end of the film, Nash explains to the Nobel Prize audience that he discovered real truth in the heart, not the head. So elevating the mind to the absolute determiner of truth leads to self-destruction. But redemption and real truth is found in human connection through love.

In *Charlie and the Chocolate Factory*, the five different kids who win tickets to tour Willy Wonka's factory become symbols of the negative results that different types of parenting bring. A suburban overachiever shows the perils of hypercompetition. A fat German boy serves as a symbol of conspicuous consumption. A spoiled little rich girl gets everything she asks for by whining. A video-game enthusiast embodies antisocial behavior. And of course, there is Charlie, whose poor but loving family sacrifices their needs for his happiness. The storyteller communicates his view of what parenting should really be like through children as symbols of different approaches.

In his letter to the Galatians, the apostle Paul allegorizes Hagar and Sarah as symbols for Jews in bondage to law and Christians as true children of Abraham (Gal 4:21-31). Jerusalem and Mount Zion itself are frequently used as symbols for the church or the people of God (Heb 12:18-24). Tax collectors are used as symbols of greed and distance from God (Mt 5:46; 11:19).

CONCLUSION

Though many of these examples of story rhetoric would be criticized as being logical fallacies, they are nevertheless used and given legitimacy in the Bible as effective means of communication and persuasion. They cannot be written off with the wave of a modernist hand as "emotional manipulation." An argument can be invalid, but its conclusion still true, and its effect powerful.

SIX

Subversion

The Bible is often image-oriented in its communication of truth. And rather than rejecting all non-Christian imagery as useless in the area of truth or persuasion, the Bible redefines such imagery in a new context of the Christian worldview. It redeems culture through subversion, which is radical reinterpretation or undermining of commonly understood images, words, concepts or narratives.

The Old Testament, a covenantal text of ancient Israel, reflects what scholar John Walton calls the "cognitive environment" of the ancient Near Eastern culture.[1] That is, God providentially breathed (inspired) his Word through human authors, who reflected thought forms and images of their surrounding culture, redefined or interpreted through their religion. This does not mean that Israel *borrowed* pagan notions or that their faith *evolved* out of other religions, but rather that all cultures within a common time and location use common imagery, symbols and mo-

---

[1]John H. Walton, *Ancient Near Eastern Thought and the Old Testament: Introducing the Conceptual World of the Hebrew Bible* (Grand Rapids: Baker, 2006), p. 21.

tifs to linguistically express their unique interpretation of reality. The writers of the Law and the Prophets of the Old Covenant are no different.

The Law given to Moses on Mount Sinai, as well as the structure of the entire Pentateuch, reflects the same structure as the pagan suzerain-vassal treaties of the ancient Near East. The creation account in Genesis 1 contains the same motifs of separation, naming and function that pervades Egyptian and Mesopotamian creation stories.[2] In the Bible, God's power and authority, as well as his creative act of bringing order out of chaos, are expressed through his battle with and domination over the large sea serpent called "Leviathan" or "Rahab" (Job 26:12-14; 41; Ps 74:12-15; Is 27:1; 51:9-10). This same motif of creation versus serpentine chaos was prevalent in Israel's surrounding pagan cultures. For example, in the Babylonian creation myth *Enuma Elish*, Marduk has a victorious battle with the dragon Tiamat. In Canaanite texts the storm god Baal battles his enemies Sea and River to establish his rule over the gods. In these cases, as well as in the Bible, a deity battles a sea monster that embodies the powers of chaos in order to establish that deity's kingly rule.[3] In Egyptian and Mesopotamian religion, the temple was considered the center of the cosmos. Its architecture and design was a microcosm that reflected the macrocosm of the universe. The temple was described as being situated on a "cosmic mountain," a holy hill where creation first began, along with a river that flowed out of the mountain as the source of eternal life.[4] So too in the Bible God's temple was a designed microcosm of the universe (Ps 78:68-

---

[2]Ibid., p. 88.
[3]Bernhard W. Anderson, *Creation Versus Chaos: The Reinterpretation of Mythical Symbolism in the Bible* (Philadelphia: Fortress, 1987), pp. 15-26.
[4]Walton, *Ancient Near Eastern Thought*, pp. 113-34.

69) on the holy hill, the cosmic Mount Zion (Ps 43:3-4; Is 2), where an Edenic river of eternal life is symbolically described as flowing out of its gates (Ezek 47:1-12).

Though these examples only scratch the surface of the common cognitive environment that Israel shared with its pagan neighbors, they also reflect Israel's subversive reinterpretation of those images, motifs and symbols through their own narrative to express a monotheistic God who condemned other gods as worthless idols and who chose Israel to be his royal priesthood to bring redemption to the lost pagan world.

The New Testament likewise engages in such reinterpretation of pagan images and symbols. The apostle Paul quotes from Jewish pseudepigrapha as well as from pagan poets in his argumentation to both believers and unbelievers. In 2 Timothy 3:8 Paul refers to Moses' opponents "Jannes and Jambres," a reference to Pharoah's magicians in Exodus 7—9, who attempted to reproduce God's miracles and plagues. But there is no mention of the names Jannes and Jambres in the entire Old Testament. So how did Paul know the names of the two magicians? The ancient church fathers Origen[5] and Ambrose claimed these names were drawn by Paul from the Jewish pseudepigraphal work entitled *Jannes and Jambres,* which describes the Exodus episode from the perspective of these two magicians—one repentant, the other unrepentant.[6] There is also a long Jewish tradition recorded in the targum of these two names.[7] In

---

[5]Origen, *Commentary* on Matthew 27:8. "Jannes and Jambres," *The International Standard Bible Encyclopedia,* ed. James Orr (1915; OakTree Software 1.0).

[6]James H. Charlesworth, ed., *The Old Testament Pseudepigrapha,* vol. 2 (New York: Doubleday, 1983), pp. 427-42.

[7]"Jewish tradition makes them sons of Balaam (*Targum of Jonathan on Num.* xxii. 22), and places their rise at the time the Pharaoh gave command to kill the first-born of Israel (Sanhedrin, f. 106a; *Sotah* 11a), and supposes them to have been teachers of Moses, the makers of the golden calf (Midrash Tanhuma, f. 115b)." "Jannes and Jambres," in Philip Schaff, *The New Schaff-Herzog Encyclopedia of*

either case, the sources are unorthodox at best, heretical at
worst.

Jude 9 describes Michael the Archangel disputing with the devil
over the body of Moses, an incident that is spoken of nowhere else
in Scripture but which appears, according to some ancient church
fathers, in a lost Jewish book called *The Assumption of Moses.*[8]
Jude also quotes an extant nonbiblical Jewish apocalyptic called
1 Enoch when he writes,

> Enoch, in the seventh generation from Adam, prophesied, say-
> ing, "Behold, the Lord came with many thousands of His holy
> ones, to execute judgment upon all, and to convict all the
> ungodly of all their ungodly deeds which they have done in
> an ungodly way, and of all the harsh things which ungodly
> sinners have spoken against Him." (Jude 14-15)

> Behold, he will arrive with ten (thousand times a thousand)
> of the holy ones in order to execute judgment upon all. He
> will destroy the wicked ones and censure all flesh on account
> of everything that they have done, that which the sinners
> and the wicked ones committed against him. *(1 Enoch 1:9)*[9]

Biblical scholars agree that *1 Enoch's* imagery and mythological
fantasy are not scriptural and in many places fanciful fiction.
But Jude quotes a particular prophecy nonetheless as a true one.

Such biblical references to nonscriptural mythology and imagery does not validate those source references as completely
true in all aspects, no more than quoting a newspaper means that

Religious Knowledge, 6:95, accessed February 4, 2008, at <www.ccel.org/ccel/
schaff/encyc06/Page_95.html>.

[8]Richard J. Bauckham, *2 Peter, Jude,* Word Biblical Commentary 50 (Waco, Tex.:
Word, 1983), pp. 73-74.

[9]James H. Charlesworth, ed., *The Old Testament Pseudepigrapha* (New York: Doubleday, 1983), 1:13-14.

paper gets all the facts right. And it doesn't invalidate biblical authority any more than acknowledging that not everything a liar says is false. But what it does validate is circumspect usage of cultural images and mythologies as connecting points with the gospel.

But the Bible doesn't merely quote *Jewish* unbiblical mythology and imagery; it also quotes *Hellenistic* cultural imagery. In 1 Corinthians 15:33 Paul quotes a common phrase of the day: "Bad company corrupts good morals." The phrase has its origin in the Greek comedic dramatist Menander's play *Thais*. Menander was known for his bawdy portrayals of private life in raunchy comedies, like the Farrelly Brothers (*There's Something About Mary*) or Sacha Baron Cohen (*Borat*).[10] Evidently, the apostle had exposed himself to the sit-coms and R-rated movies of his day. Elsewhere, Paul depicts the persecution sufferings of the faithful as a "theatrical spectacle" to the audience of the world—original reality show programming (1 Cor 4:9; Heb 10:33).[11]

And speaking of spectacles, in Philippians 3:13-14 and 1 Corinthians 9:24-27, the publicly familiar Roman or Isthmian athletic games are used as another incarnate picture of the race and fight of Christian faith. The triumphal procession of Roman emperors dragging their defeated foes through the city streets is reimagined as a visual metaphor for Christ's own victory in 2 Corinthians 2:14-16 and Colossians 2:15.[12]

---

[10]Raymond F Collins and Donald P. Senior, *First Corinthians* (Collegeville, Minn.: Liturgical Press, 1999), pp. 560-61; Victor Davis Hanson and John Heath, *Who Killed Homer? The Demise of Classical Education and the Recovery of Greek Wisdom* (New York: Encounter Books, 2001), pp. 124, 148-49.

[11]"Theater," *Dictionary of Biblical Imagery*, AGES Software.

[12]"Classifying Convergence Between Pagan and Early Christian Texts: 2.8 Adaptation," *The Dictionary of New Testament Background*, Ages Software.

ACTS 17: PAUL AT THE AREOPAGUS

Athens was the Los Angeles or New York of its time, the place where new ideas were explored with great passion by the Greek and Roman poets, the cultural leaders of the ancient world. The poets would espouse philosophy not merely through didactical tracts and ora-

Paul in Athens, by Julius Schnorr von Carolsfeld

tion but also through poems and plays for the populace, just as the popular artists of today propagate pagan worldviews through music, television and feature films.

Paul's Areopagus discourse has been used to justify opposing theories of apologetics by Christian crosscultural evangelists, theologians and apologists alike. It has been used to justify such divergent theories of apologetics as evidentialism and presuppositionalism.[13] It has been interpreted as being a Hellenistic (i.e., culturally Greek) sermon as well as being entirely antithetical to Hellenism. Martin Dibelius concludes,

> The point at issue is whether it is the Old Testament view of history or the philosophical—Stoic—view of the world that prevails in the speech on the Areopagus. The difference of opinion that we find among the commentators seems to offer little prospect of a definite solution.[14]

One thing that most all of these divergent viewpoints have in common is their modernist emphasis on Paul's discourse as rational debate or empirical proof. What they tend to miss is the narrative structure of his presentation. And perhaps it is the narrative structure that contains the solution to Dibelius' dilemma. An examination of that structure reveals that Paul does not so much engage in dialectic as he does retell the pagan story within a Christian worldview framework.

First, our examination must put Paul's presentation in context. He is brought to the Areopagus, which was not merely the name of a location but also the name of the administrative and judicial body that met there, the highest court in Athens. The Areopagus formally examined and charged violators of the Roman law against "illicit" new religions.[15] Though the context suggests an open public interaction and not a formal trial, Luke, the nar-

---

[13]Evidentialism is the belief that sinners can be persuaded to faith through evidence of the historical reliability of the Bible, the miracles and the resurrection of Jesus. Presuppositionalism is the belief that evidence does not persuade sinners because all evidence is interpreted through the presuppositions (assumptions) of their worldview. Unbelievers therefore should be persuaded through addressing their worldviews and presuppositions.

[14]Martin Dibelius and K. C. Hanson, *The Book of Acts: Form, Style, and Theology* (1956; reprint, Minneapolis: Augsburg Fortress, 2004), p. 98.

[15]Robert L. Gallagher and Paul Hertig, *Mission in Acts: Ancient Narratives in Contemporary Context* (Maryknoll, N.Y.: Orbis, 2004), pp. 224-25.

rator, attempts to cast Paul in Athenian narrative simile to Socrates, someone with whom the Athenians would be both familiar and uncomfortable. Luke describes the reaction of some of the philosophers on hand to Paul in verse 18: "He seems to be a proclaimer of strange deities," a phrase that resembles Xenophon's description of Socrates' crime: "rejecting the gods acknowledged by the state and . . . bringing in new divinities."[16] Luke depicts Paul from the start as a heroically defiant Socrates, a philosopher of truth against the mob.

Paul's sermon clearly contains biblical truths that are found in both Old and New Testaments: God as transcendent Creator and Sustainer, his providential control of reality, Christ's resurrection and the final judgment. It is highly significant to note,

The Acropolis

however, that throughout the entire discourse Paul did not quote a single Scripture to these unbelievers. Paul certainly was not ashamed of the gospel and regularly quoted Scriptural references to the Jewish people (Acts 26:22-23; 28:23-28); there-

---

[16]Xenophon *Memorabilia* chap. 1. See also Plato *Apology* 24B-C; *Euthyphro* 1C; 2B; 3B.

fore, his avoidance of Scripture in this instance is instructive of how to preach and defend the gospel to pagans. Quoting chapter and verse may work with those who are already disposed toward God or the Bible, but Paul appears to consider it inappropriate to do so with those who are hostile or opposed to the faith. Ben Witherington adds, "Arguments are only persuasive if they work within the plausibility structure existing in the minds of the hearers."[17] Paul, rather than Bible-thumping these heathens, addresses them using the narrative structure of Stoic philosophy.[18]

Missions scholars Robert Gallagher and Paul Hertig explain that the facts of Paul's speech mimic the major points of Stoic beliefs. They quote the ancient Roman academic Cicero who outlines these Stoic beliefs:

> First, they prove that gods exist; next they explain their nature; then they show that the world is governed by them; and lastly that they care for the fortunes of mankind.[19]

Paul enters into the discourse of his listeners. He plays according to the rules of the community he is trying to reach. An examination of each point he makes in his oration will reveal that this identification he is making with their culture is not merely with their structural *procedures* of argument, but with

---

[17]Ben Witherington III, *The Acts of the Apostles: A Socio-Rhetorical Commentary* (Grand Rapids: Eerdmans, 1998), p. 530.

[18]This raises the spectre of the centuries-long debate over natural theology. Can sinners be persuaded by the natural revelation of unaided reason or must they hear the special revelation of God's Scriptures to be saved? Paul certainly here speaks of special revelation when he mentions the resurrection of Christ and the final judgment. But he does so *without* Scriptural reference. So the real question is: Must one quote Bible chapter and verse to speak special revelation? Evidently not, according to Paul.

[19]Cicero *On the Nature of the Gods* 2.4, cited in Gallagher and Hertig, *Mission in Acts*, p. 230.

the *content* of the Stoic worldview. He is retelling the Stoic story through a Christian metanarrative.[20]

Paul begins his address with a rhetorical convention among Athenians, noted by such luminary Greeks as Aristotle and Demosthenes:[21]

Men of Athens, I observe that you are very religious in all respects. (Acts 17:22)

He affirms their religiosity, which also had been acknowledged by the famous Athenian dramatist Sophocles: "Athens is held of states, the most devout"; as well as the Greek geographer Pausanias: "Athenians more than others venerate the gods."[22]

Paul goes on:

While I was passing through and examining the objects of your worship, I also found an altar with this inscription, "TO AN UNKNOWN GOD." Therefore what you worship in ignorance, this I proclaim to you. (Acts 17:23)

The "Unknown God" inscription may have been the Athenian attempt to hedge their bets against any god they may have missed paying homage to out of ignorance.[23] Paul quoted the ambiguous text as a point of departure for reflections on true worship, which was the same conventional technique used by Pseudo-Heraclitus in his *Fourth Epistle*.[24]

---

[20]Although the text reveals that both Epicureans and Stoics were there (Acts 17:17-18), it appears that Paul chooses Stoicism to identify with, perhaps because of its closer affinity with the elements of his intended message.

[21]Aristotle *Pan. Or.* 1, Demosthenes *Exordia* 54, cited in Witherington, *Acts of the Apostles,* p. 520.

[22]Sophocles *Oedipus Tyrannus* 260, Pausanias *Description of Greece* 1.17.1, cited in Charles H. Talbert, *Reading Acts: A literary and Theological Commentary on the Acts of the Apostles* (Macon, Ga.: Smyth & Helwys, 2001), p. 53.

[23]Dibelius and Hanson, *Book of Acts,* p. 103.

[24]Talbert, *Reading Acts,* p. 153.

Paul continues:

The God who made the world and all things in it, since He is Lord of heaven and earth, does not dwell in temples made with hands; nor is He served by human hands, as though He needed anything, since He Himself gives to all people life and breath and all things. (Acts 17:24-25)

The Greeks had many sacred temples throughout the ancient world as houses for their gods. The Stoics and other cultural critics, however, considered such attempts at housing the transcendent incorporeal nature of deity to be laughable. Zeno, the founder of Stoicism, was known to have taught that "temples are not to be built to the gods."[25] Euripides, the celebrated Athenian tragedian, foreshadowed Paul's own words with the rhetorical question, "What house fashioned by builders could contain the divine form within enclosed walls?"[26] Paul's contemporary, the Stoic philosopher Seneca, was known to have said, "Temples are not to be built to Him with stones piled up on high."[27]

The Hebrew tradition also carried such repudiation of a physical dwelling place for God (1 Kings 8:27; Is 66:1-2), but the context of Paul's speech rings particularly sympathetic to the Stoics residing in the midst of the sacred hill of the Athenian Acropolis,

[25]Explained of Zeno by Plutarch in his *Moralia* 1034B, as cited in Juhana Torkki, *The Dramatic Account of Paul's Encounter with Philosophy: An Analysis of Acts 17:16-34 with Regard to Contemporary Philosophical Debates* (Academic diss., Helsinki University Printing House, 2004), p. 105.

[26]Euripedes, fragment 968, cited in F. F. Bruce, *Paul Apostle of the Heart Set Free* (1977; reprint, Cumbria, U.K.: Paternoster, 2000), p. 240.

[27]According to Lactantius *Institutes* 6.25, cited in Talbert, *Reading Acts*, p. 155.

populated by a multitude of temples such as the Parthenon, the Erechtheion, the Temple of Nike and the Athenia Polias.

The idea that God does not need humankind, but that humankind needs God as his creator and sustainer (Acts 17:25) is common enough in Hebrew thought (Ps 50:9-12), but as Dibelius points out,

> The use of the word "serve" is, however, almost unknown in the Greek translation of the Bible, but quite familiar in original Greek (pagan) texts, and in the context with which we are acquainted. The deity is too great to need my "service," we read in the famous chapter of Xenophon's *Memorabilia*, which contains the teleological proof of God.... From the Eleatic School onwards, the idea that God is not in need of anything is repeated in all the schools of Greek philosophy till the Neo-Pythagoreans and the Neo-Platonists.[28]

Seneca wrote, "God seeks no servants; He himself serves mankind," which is also reflected in Euripides' claim that "God has need of nothing," and Plutarch's "God is self-sufficient."[29] Paul is striking a familiar chord with the Athenian and Stoic narratives.

He made from one man every nation of mankind to live on all the face of the earth. (Acts 17:26)

Cicero noted that the "universal brotherhood of mankind"[30] was a common theme in Stoicism—although when Stoics spoke of "man" they tended to exclude the barbarians surrounding them.[31] Nevertheless, as Seneca observed, "Nature produced us related to

---

[28]Dibelius and Hanson, *Book of Acts*, pp. 105-6.

[29]Seneca *Epistle* 95.47; Euripides *Hercules* 1345-46; Plutarch *Moralia* 1052D, as cited in Talbert, *Reading Acts*, p. 155.

[30]Cicero *On Duties* 3.6.28, quoted in Michelle V. Lee, *Paul, the Stoics, and the Body of Christ* (Cambridge: Cambridge University Press, 2006), p. 88.

[31]Bruce, *Paul*, p. 241.

one another, since she created us from the same source and to the same end."[32] The Athenians would certainly not be thinking of the Hebrew Adam when they heard that reference to "one." The "one" they would be thinking of would be the gods themselves. Seneca wrote, "All persons, if they are traced back to their origins, are descendents of the gods," and Dio Chrysostom affirmed, "It is from the gods that the race of men is sprung."[33] What is also striking in Paul's dialogue is that he neglects to mention Adam as the "one" from which we are created, something he readily did when writing to the Roman Christians (Rom 5:12-21). Paul may have been deliberately ambiguous at this point by not distinguishing his definition of "one" from the Greeks', in order to maintain consistency with the Stoic Greek narrative. He is undermining Stoicism through the Christian worldview, which will be confirmed conclusively in a climactic plot twist at the end of his narrative.

. . . having determined their appointed times and the boundaries of their habitation. (Acts 17:26)

Christians may read Acts 17:26 and immediately consider it an expression of God's providential sovereignty over history, as in Genesis 1, where God determines the times and seasons, or in Deuteronomy 32:8, where he separates the sons of men and establishes their "boundaries." But Paul's Athenian audience would refer to their own intellectual heritage on hearing these words. As Juhana Torkki points out, "The idea of God's kinship to humans is unique in the New Testament writings but common in Stoicism. The Stoic (philosopher) Epictetus devoted a whole essay to the subject."[34] In that essay, Epictetus writes:

---

[32]Quoted in Lee, *Paul, the Stoics, and the Body of Christ*, p. 84.
[33]Seneca *Epistle* 44.1; Dio Chrysostom *Oration* 30.26, as cited in Talbert, *Reading Acts*, p. 156.
[34]Torkki, *Dramatic Account of Paul's Encounter with Philosophy*, p. 87.

When he tells plants to bloom, they bloom, when he tells them to bear fruit, they bear it, when he tells them to ripen, they ripen. . . . Is God (Zeus) then, not capable of overseeing everything and being present with everything and maintaining a certain distribution with everything?[35]

Cicero, in one of his *Tusculan Disputations*, writes that seasons and zones of habitation are evidence of God's existence.[36] Paul continues, with every sentence Luke narrates, to engage Stoic thought by retelling its narrative.

That they would seek God, if perhaps they might grope for Him and find Him, though He is not far from each one of us. (Acts 17:27)

The image in Acts 17:27, as one commentator explains, "carries the sense of 'a blind person or the fumbling of a person

in the darkness of night,'" as can be found in the writings of Aristophanes and Plato.[37] Christian apologist Greg Bahnsen suggests that it may even be an Homeric literary allusion to the Cyclops blindly groping for Odysseus and his men. [38] In any case, the image is not a positive one. F. F. Bruce affirms the Hellenistic affinities of this section by quoting the Stoic Dio Chrysostom. "Primaeval men are described as 'not settled separately by themselves far away from the di-

[35]Epictetus *Discourse* 1.14, quoted in A. A. Long, *Epictetus: A Stoic and Socratic Guide to Life* (Oxford: Oxford University Press, 2002), pp. 25-26.

[36]Cicero *Tusculan Disputations* 1.28.68-69, as cited in Talbert, *Reading Acts*, p. 156.

[37]Aristophanes *Ec.* 315; *Pax* 691; Plato *Phaedo* 99b, cited in Witherington, *Acts of the Apostles*, pp. 528-29.

[38]Greg Bahnsen, *Always Ready: Directions for Defending the Faith*, ed. Robert Booth (Atlanta: American Vision, 1996), pp. 260-61.

vine being or outside him, but . . . sharing his nature.'"[39] Seneca, true to Stoic form, wrote, "God is near you, He is with you, He is within you."[40]

This idea of humanity, blindly groping around for what is, in fact, very near is also a part of scriptural themes (Is 59:10; Deut 28:29), but with a distinct difference. To the Stoic, God's nearness was a pantheistic nearness. They believed everything was a part of God and God was a part of everything, something Paul would vehemently deny (Rom 1) but, interestingly enough, does not do so at this point. He continues to maintain a surface connection with the Stoics by affirming the immanence of God without explicitly qualifying it.

Paul thus far has implicitly followed the Stoic narrative without qualifying the differences between it and his full narrative. He now, however, becomes more explicit in identifying with these pagans, favorably quoting some of their own poets to affirm even more identity with them.

> For in Him we live and move and exist, as even some of your own poets have said, "For we also are His children." (Acts 17:28)

"In him we live and move and exist" is a line from Epimenides' well-known *Cretica*:

> They fashioned a tomb for thee, / O holy and high one— / But thou art not dead; / thou livest and abidest for ever / for, *in thee we live and move and have our being.*[41]

[39]Dio Chrysostom *Olympic Oration* 12:28, cited in F. F. Bruce, *The Book of the Acts*, New International Commentary on the New Testament, rev. ed. (Grand Rapids: Eerdmans, 1988), p. 339.

[40]Seneca *Epistle* 41.1-2, cited in Talbert, *Reading Acts*, p. 156.

[41]Bruce, *Book of the Acts*, pp. 338-39.

"We are his offspring," is from Epimenides' fellow-countryman Aratus in his *Phaenomena:*

> Let us begin with Zeus, Never, O men, let us leave him
> Unmentioned. All the ways are full of Zeus,
> And all the market-places of human beings. The sea is full
> Of him; so are the harbors. In every way we have all to do
>   with Zeus,
> *For we are truly his offspring.*[42]

Aratus was most likely rephrasing Cleanthes' poem *Hymn to Zeus,* which not only refers to men as God's children, but to Zeus as

the sovereign controller of all—in whom men live and move:

> Almighty Zeus, nature's first Cause,
>   governing all things by law.
> It is the right of mortals to address thee,
> For we *who live and creep upon the earth are*
>   *all thy children.*[43]

These are the same elements of Paul's discourse in Acts 17:24-29.

The Stoics themselves had redefined Zeus to be the impersonal pantheistic force, also called the "logos," as opposed to a personal deity in the pantheon of Greek gods.[44] This *logos* was still not anything like the personal God of the Hebrew Scriptures. What is disturbing about this section is that Paul does not qualify the

---

[42]Ibid.

[43]C. Loring Brace, *Unknown God, Or Inspiration Among Pre-Christian Races 1890* (Whitefish, Mt.: Kessinger, 2003), p. 123.

[44]Joseph Lienhard, *The Bible, the Church, and Authority: The Canon of the Christian Bible in History and Theology* (Collegeville, Minn: Liturgical Press, 1995), p. 11.

pagan quotations that originally were directed to Zeus. He doesn't clarify by explaining that Zeus is not the God he is talking about. He simply quotes these hymns of praise to Zeus as if they are in agreement with the Christian gospel. The question arises, why does he not distinguish his gospel narrative from theirs?

The answer is found in the idea of subversion. Paul is subverting their concept of God by using common terms with a different definition that eventually undermines their entire narrative. He begins with their conventional understanding of God but steers them eventually to his own. The *imago dei* (image of God) in pagans reflects distorted truth, but a kind of truth nonetheless.

Now Paul turns his attention to idolatry.

We ought not to think that the Divine Nature is like gold or silver or stone, an image formed by the art and thought of man. (Acts 17:29)

The Stoics believed that the divine nature could not be reducible to mere artifacts of humanity's creation. Epictetus called humans a "fragment of God."

You have within you a part of Him. . . . Do you suppose that I am speaking of some external God, made of silver or gold? It is within yourself that you bear Him.[45]

Zeno taught that "men shall neither build temples nor make idols"; Dio Chrysostom wrote, "The living can only be represented by something that is living."[46] Paul is addressing

---

[45]Epictetus *Discourses* 2.8.11-12, cited in Gallagher, *Mission in Acts*, p. 232.
[46]Clement of Alexandria *Miscellanies* 5.76; Dio Chrysostom *Oration* 12.83, cited in

the biblical mocking of "idols of silver and gold" (Ps 115:4) in language his hearers would understand: the language of the Stoic narrative.

Paul goes on.

Therefore having overlooked the times of ignorance, God is now declaring to men that all people everywhere should repent, because He has fixed a day in which He will judge the world in righteousness through a Man whom He has appointed, having furnished proof to all men by raising Him from the dead. (Acts 17:30-31)

For the Stoics, ignorance was an important doctrine. It represented the loss of knowledge that man formerly possessed, knowledge of their pantheistic unity with the *logos*. Dio Chrysostom asks in his *Discourses*, "How, then, could they have remained ignorant and conceived no inkling . . . (that) they were filled with the divine nature?"[47] Epictetus echoes the same sentiment: "Why then are you ignorant of your own kinship? . . . You are bearing God about with you, you poor wretch, and know it not!"[48] Pauline "ignorance" was a willing responsible ignorance, a hardness of heart that came from sinful violation of God's commands (Eph 4:17-19)— but yet again, Paul does not articulate this distinction. He instead makes an ambiguous reference to a generic "ignorance" that the Stoics would most naturally interpret in their own terms. As Talbert describes, "In all of this, he has sought the common ground. There is nothing he has said yet that would appear ridiculous to his philosophic audience."[49]

Talbert, *Reading Acts,* p. 156.

[47]Dio Chrysostom *Discourses* 12.27; cf. 12.12, 16, 21, cited in Gallagher, *Mission in Acts,* p. 229.

[48]Epictetus *Discourses* 2.8.11-14, cited in Gallagher, *Mission in Acts,* p. 229.

[49]Talbert, *Reading Acts,* p. 156.

Here is where the subversion of Paul's storytelling rears its head, like the mind-blowing
twist of a movie thriller. Everything is not as
it seems. Paul the storyteller got his pagan audience to nod their heads in agreement, only to
be thrown for a loop at the end. Repentance,
judgment and the resurrection, all antithetical to Stoic beliefs, form the conclusion of

Paul's narrative. Witherington concludes of this Areopagus speech
surprise ending,

> Greek notions have been taken up and given new meaning by
> placing them in a Jewish-Christian monotheistic context.
> Apologetics by means of defense and attack is being done, us-
> ing Greek thought to make monotheistic points. The call for
> repentance at the end shows where the argument has been go-
> ing all along—it is not an exercise in diplomacy or compro-
> mise but ultimately a call for conversion.[50]

The Stoics believed in a "great conflagration" of fire where
the universe would end in the same kind of fire out of which it was
created.[51] This was not the fire of damnation, as in Christian doctrine. It was rather the cyclical recurrence of what scientists
today would call the "oscillating universe." Everything would
collapse into fire, and then be recreated again out of that fire
and relive the same process and development of history all over
again: The same Socrates would be reborn and would suffer again
the betrayal of his city-state and drink the hemlock yet again.
And this would occur over and over again from fire into fire and
back again.

---

[50]Witherington, *Acts of the Apostles,* p. 524.
[51]Ibid., p. 526.

Paul's call of final, noncyclical, once-for-all judgment by a man was certainly one of the factors that caused some of these interested philosophers to scorn him (Acts 17:32). Yet note again that even here, Paul does not give the name of Jesus. He alludes to him and implies his identity, which seems to maintain a sense of mystery about the narrative (something modern evangelists would surely criticize). At times, silence can be louder than words, and implication can be more alluring than explication.

The other factor sure to provoke the ire of the cosmopolitan Athenian culture-shapers was the proclamation of the resurrection of Jesus. The poet/ dramatist Aeschylus wrote what became a prominent Stoic slogan, "When the dust has soaked up a man's blood, once he is dead there is no resurrection." [52] So Paul's explicit reference to the resurrection was certainly a part of the twist that he used in his subversive storytelling to get the Athenians to listen to what they might otherwise ignore.

A couple of important observations are in line regarding Paul's reference to pagan poetry and non-Christian mythology. First, it points out that, as an orthodox Pharisee who stressed separation of holiness, he nevertheless did not consider it unholy to expose himself to the godless media and art forms of his day (books, plays and poetry). He did not merely familiarize himself with them, he *studied* them—well enough to be able to quote them and even utilize their narrative. Yes, Paul primarily quoted Scripture in his writings, but he also quoted sinners favorably when appropriate.

Second, this appropriation of pagan cultural images and

---

[52]Cited in Bruce, *Paul: Apostle of the Heart Set Free,* p. 247.

STOIC IDEA	ACTS 17
Incorporeal nature of God	v. 24-25
God's self-sufficiency	v. 25
Brotherhood of man "oneness"	v. 26
Providence over seasons and habitations	v. 26
Man's blind groping	v. 27
Immanence/Pantheism	v. 27-28
Zeus/Logos	v. 28
Man as God's offspring	v. 28
Divine nature not gold or silver	v. 29
Wisdom versus ignorance	v. 23, 30
Justice	v. 30-31

Figure 6.1. Stoic ideas converge in Acts 17. See "Historical Sketch of Ethics: Stoicism and Paul," in *The International Standard Bible Encyclopedia*, ed. James Orr (1915; OakTree Software 1.0).

thought forms by biblical writers reflects more than mere quoting of popular sayings or shallow cultural reference. It illustrates a redemptive interaction with those thought forms, a certain amount of involvement in and affirmation of the prevailing culture, in service to the gospel. A comparison of Paul's sermon in Acts 17 with Cleanthes' *Hymn to Zeus,* a well-known summary of Stoic doctrine, reveals an almost point-by-point correspondence of ideas, which certainly suggests a deliberate identification by Paul with the narrative of the Stoics, while not ultimately compromising the gospel.[53] The list of convergences between the Mars Hill discourse and Stoic ideas are summarized in figure 6.1.

The *Dictionary of New Testament Background* cites over a hundred New Testament passages that reflect convergence between pa-

[53]See M. A. C. Ellery, trans., *Hymn to Zeus* (1976), accessed February 5, 2008, at <www.utexas.edu/courses/citylife/readings/cleanthes_hymn.html>.

gan and early Christian texts. Citations, images and word pictures are quoted, adapted or appropriated from such pagans as Aeschylus, Sophocles, Plutarch, Tacitus, Xenophon, Aristotle, Seneca and other Hellenistic cultural sources. The sheer volume of such biblical reference suggests an interactive intercourse of Scriptural writings with culture rather than absolute separation or shallow manipulation of that culture.[54] Some Christians may react with fear that this kind of redemptive interaction with culture is syncretism, an attempt to fuse two incompatible systems of thought. Subversion, however, is not syncretism. And subversion is what Paul was engaged in.

SYNCRETISM VERSUS SUBVERSION

In subversion, the narrative, images and symbols of one system are discreetly redefined or altered in the new system. Thus Paul quotes a poem to Zeus but covertly intends a different deity. He superficially affirms the immanence of the Stoic "Universal Reason" that controls and determines all nature and men, yet he describes this universal all-powerful deity as personal rather than abstract law. He agrees with the Stoics that men are ignorant of God and his justice, but then affirms God will judge the world because of Christ's resurrection—two doctrines the Stoics were vehemently against. He affirms the unity of humanity and the immanence of God in all things, but he contradicts Stoic pantheism and redefines that immanence by affirming God's transcendence and the creature/Creator distinction. Paul did not reveal these stark differences between the gospel and the Stoic narrative until the end of his talk. Paul was subverting pa-

---

[54]*Dictionary of New Testament Background* (2000; OakTree Software 1.0).

ganism, not syncretizing Christianity with it.

By casting his presentation of the gospel in terms that Stoics could identify with and by undermining their narrative with alterations, Paul was strategically subverting through story. In his book *Engaging Unbelief*, Curtis Chang explains this rhetorical strategy as threefold: "1. Entering the challenger's story, 2. Retelling the story, 3. Capturing that retold tale with the gospel metanarrative."[55] Chang affirms the inescapability of story and image through history even in philosophical argumentation:

> Strikingly, many of the classic philosophical arguments
> from different traditions seem to take the form of a story:
> from Plato's scene of the man bound to the chair in the cave
> to Hobbes's elaborate drama of the "state of nature," to John
> Rawls's "choosing game." Stories may come in many different
> genres, but we cannot escape them.[56]

Many Christian apologists and theologians have tended to focus on the doctrinal content of Paul's Areopagus speech, and therefore miss the narrative structure that carries the message. There is certainly more proclamation in this passage than rational argument. Paul's narrative mirrors the beginning, middle and end of linear Western storytelling. God is Lord. He created all things, all people from one (creation), then determined the seasons and boundaries. Men became blind and are groping in the darkness, ignorant of their very identity as his children (fall). God raised a man from the dead and will judge the world in the future through that same man. Through repentance, people can escape their ignorance and separation from God (redemption).

---

[55]Curtis Chang, *Engaging Unbelief: A Captivating Strategy from Augustine to Aquinas* (Downers Grove, Ill.: InterVarsity Press, 2000), p. 26.
[56]Ibid, p. 30.

Scholar N. T. Wright suggests that the way to handle the clash
of competing stories is to tell yet another story; one that encom-
passes and explains the opposing stories yet contains an explanation for the anomalies or contradictions within those stories.

There is no such thing as "neutral" or "objective" proof;
only the claim that the story we are now telling about the
world as a whole makes more sense, in its outline and detail,
than other potential or actual stories that may be on offer.
Simplicity of outline, elegance in handling the details
within it, the inclusion of all the parts of the story, and the
ability of the story to make sense beyond its immediate sub-
ject-matter: these are what count.[57]

The claim that we observe evidence objectively and apply reason neutrally to prove our worldview is an artifact of Enlightenment mythology. The truth is that each epoch of thought in history, whether medieval, Enlightenment or postmodern, is a contest
in storytelling. "The one who can tell the best story, in a very
real sense, wins the epoch."[58] That's what Paul does with the
Stoics.

The conventional image of a Christian apologist is one who
teaches at a university, one who wields logical arguments for the
existence of God and manuscript evidence for the reliability of
the Bible, one who engages in debates about evolution or Islam. But
in a postmodern world focused on narrative discourse, we need to
take a lesson from the apostle Paul and expand our avenues for
evangelism and defending the faith. We need more Christian apologists writing revisionist biographies of Darwin, Marx and Freud;

---

[57]N. T. Wright, *The New Testament and the People of God* (Minneapolis: Fortress, 1992), p. 42.
[58]Ibid., p. 29.

writing for and subverting pagan TV sitcoms; bringing a Christian worldview to their journalism in secular magazines and news reporting; making horror films that undermine the idol of modernity; playing subversive industrial, rock and rap music. We need to be actively, sacredly subverting the secular stories of the culture, and restoring their fragmented narratives for Christ. If it was good enough for the apostle Paul on top of Mars Hill, then it's certainly good enough for those of us in the shade of the Hollywood hills now.

SEVEN

Cultural Captivity

The New Testament book of Hebrews has long been recognized by Bible scholars as reflecting a subversive interaction with the Hellenism of the first century. A famous Alexandrian Jewish writer of the time period, Philo, had attempted to integrate Platonic philosophy with Judaism. The result was a form of Hellenism that was very influential on the Jews and Christians of the day. One of the many doctrinal beliefs of this school was that the spiritual world of "ideas" was good and more real than the physical world, which was inherently evil and shadowlike. Hellenistic Judaism believed, with Plato, that the body is a prison house of the soul that longed to be released so it could become perfect and return to its maker, the Logos (Reason) or Sophia (wisdom). Since the physical world was bad and the spiritual world was good, a chasm separated humans from God.

Because of the ontological gap between man and God, Philo wrote of various mediators for man such as angels, Moses, Melchizedek, and the high priest. Hellenism posited that the world was created through the agency of the Logos, as the "firstborn son" who was also "light," a media-tory being on the borderline between Godhood and man.[1] The Hellenistic apocryphal book *The Wisdom of Solomon* speaks of Divine Wisdom mediating God's revelation, creating and sustaining the world, and reconciling men to God (7:21—8:1)—all elements related to Jesus in the book of Hebrews, but written to Hellenistic Jews.

The description of Jesus as Logos, Sophia and creator and sustainer of the world in the book of Hebrews, however, diametrically opposes these essential doctrines of the Platonic philosophy. The incarnation of Christ, God in the flesh (Heb 2:17) being tempted by sin (Heb 4:15) and experiencing suffering and other passions (Heb 5:7) was entirely incompatible with the Platonic notion of God's complete separation from humanity and physical reality. The writer of Hebrews connects with certain Hellenis-

The Baptism of Jesus, by Julius Schnorr von Carolsfeld

[1]Ronald Nash, *The Gospel and the Greeks: Did the New Testament Borrow from Pagan Thought?* (Phillipsburg, N.J.: P & R Publishing, 1992, 2003), pp. 81-82.

tic notions of Logos and Sophia and then subverts them with the incarnational Logos of Scripture.

The book of Hebrews describes Jesus as superior to each of Philo's mediators one by one: angels (Heb 1:1-14), Moses (Heb 3:1-18), Melchizedek (Heb 5:1-10) and the high priest (Heb 5:1-10), thus subverting the Hellenistic notions of mediatorship.[2] Ronald Nash concludes in *The Gospel and the Greeks,*

> What becomes clear in a study of Hebrews is not that the writer was unfamiliar with Platonism, but that he self-consciously and intentionally set himself to contrast his understanding of the Christian message with the philosophy that he himself may have once accepted and that his audience may still have found attractive.[3]

So the book of Hebrews reflects the language, terms and concepts of Hellenism, but undermines them with new definitions of terms and usage. Similarly, the Gospel of John uses language that subverts Hellenistic mystery religion. In the very first chapter, John uses a word to define Jesus (*logos*) that was well known in the dominant Hellenistic culture as a reference to Reason as the underlying structural order of all things. A look at a couple fragments from Heraclitus, the possible origin of the concept, will shed some light on just how the Greco-Roman pagans of John's era defined this "Logos."

> When you have listened, not to me, but to the [Logos], it is wise to agree that all things are one.
>
> For though all things come into being in accordance with this Logos, men seem as if they have never met it.[4]

One can read the first verses of the Gospel of John and see its obvious

[2]Nash, *Gospel and the Greeks,* pp. 94-98.
[3]Ibid., p. 90.
[4]James B. Wilbur and Harold J. Allen, *The Worlds of the Early Greek Philosophers* (Buffalo, N.Y.: Prometheus Books, 1979), pp. 64-65.

identification with this Greco-Roman concept of Logos.

> In the beginning was the Word [*logos*], and the Word [*logos*] was
> with God, and the Word [*logos*] was God. He was in the beginning
> with God. All things came into being through Him, and apart from
> Him nothing came into being that has come into being. In Him
> was life, and the life was the Light of men. The Light shines in the
> darkness, and the darkness did not comprehend it. . . . And the
> Word [*logos*] became flesh, and dwelt among us, and we saw His
> glory, glory as of the only begotten from the Father, full of grace
> and truth. (Jn 1:1-5, 14)

John's definition of the Logos, however, shows a subversion taking place. For Greek philosophy, the Logos affirmed the oneness of all things out of which all things were created and separated. Men were ignorant of this knowledge but enlightened by it because the Logos was pure thought itself as an intelligent guiding force.[5] When John wrote his Gospel, he started with Logos rather than the Hebrew name YHWH or the Greek equivalents *Kyrios* or *Theos* as the creator of the universe. He echoed the Greek philosophical language of ultimate origin, immanence, lightness and darkness, human ignorance and the "fullness" of truth, but he gave it a Hebrew spin. John's Logos is not an abstract force but a rational person. The Greek understanding of ultimate reality is shown to be inadequate in light of Christianity.

The apostle Peter subverts Hellenistic imagery when he writes about the cataclysmic spiritual events surrounding God's judgment in the Noachian flood.

> God did not spare angels when they sinned, but cast them into hell
> and committed them to pits of darkness, reserved for judgment. (2
> Pet 2:4)

---

[5]Ibid., p. 63.

What is important to realize is that the word translated as "hell" in this English translation is not the usual Greek word, *gehenna,* but *tartarus,* a well-known Greek mythic location written about by Plato:

> The very wicked are cast for ever into Tartarus, the traditional place of punishment in Hades surrounded by a brazen wall and encircled by impenetrable darkness. Here, they receive terrible torture (*Republic* 626).[6]

The Greek poet Hesiod, writing around 700 B.C., described Tartarus as the underworld pit of darkness and gloom where the Olympian Titan giants were banished following their war with Zeus.[7] Obviously, Peter does not affirm Greco-Roman polytheism by referring to Tartarus, but he is clearly using a Hellenistic word that his readers, believer and unbeliever alike, would be very familiar with, and he redefines it within his Christian faith.[8]

GOSPEL VERSUS EMPIRE

The Roman Emperor was considered deity, and all Roman subjects were required to pay homage in worship to him. And when an emperor would

Caesar Augustus

conquer a particular ruler, he would strip that ruler of his weapons and armor and drag him in chains, along with the captured spoils of war, in a "triumphal procession" through the streets of

---

[6]"Resurrection," in *New International Dictionary of New Testament Theology,* ed. Colin Brown (Grand Rapids: Zondervan, 1975, 1986; OakTree Software 1.0).

[7]"Polytheism, Greco-Roman," in *Dictionary of New Testament Background* (Downers Grove, Ill.: InterVarsity Press, 2000; OakTree Software 1.0).

[8]Some scholars suggest that the Greek notion of giants in Tartarus is actually a distorted pagan retelling of the much earlier biblical story of the imprisonment of giants or fallen angels during the Noachian flood (Gen 6:1-7). This would then be an example of paganism subverting Judeo-Christianity, which Peter then subverts right back.

the city.[9] Paul describes the spiritual victory of Christ's atonement in exactly these imperial terms:

> When He had disarmed the rulers and authorities, He made a public display of them, having triumphed over them through Him. (Col 2:15)

> But thanks be to God, who always leads us in triumph in Christ. (2 Cor 2:14)

In these passages, Paul is claiming for Jesus the prerogatives of Caesar, reducing Caesar's own power to mere parody of Christ's greater authority. N. T. Wright points out that even preaching the gospel is presented in the Scriptures as a "herald of good news" (Lk 16:16) of Christ's kingdom and rule over all other human authorities on the earth. This reflects not only the Hebrew concept of "good news" (Is 52:7) but a subversion of Roman practice: a herald announcing "as good news" the birth or rule of the emperor as a savior to all the world.[10]

When Paul wrote that "our citizenship is in heaven, from which also we eagerly wait for a Savior, the Lord Jesus Christ" (Phil 3:20), he was subversively defying the concept of Roman citizenship as the ultimate obligation on occupied territories. Ancient Roman sources call Caesar "the savior and benefactor of the inhabited world,"[11] the one who brought a new world of salvation, justice and peace.[12] Jesus is subversively portrayed in the image of the Roman Emperor, in effect, stealing Caesar's thunder.[13]

---

[9]*Barnes' Notes on the New Testament*, derived from an electronic text from the Christian Classics Ethereal Library (www.ccel.org), formatted and corrected by OakTree 1.0.

[10]N. T. Wright, *What Saint Paul Really Said* (Grand Rapids: Eerdmans, 1997), pp. 42-45. Wright quotes a Roman inscription of 9 B.C. that refers to the birth of Emperor Augustus as providence sending "a *saviour* for us and those who came after us, *to make war to cease, to create order everywhere* ... the birthday of the god [Augustus] was the beginning for the world of the *good news* that have come to men through him."

[11]Accessed February 5, 2008, at <www.bsw.org/project/biblica/bibl79/Comm05m.htm>.

[12]Richard A. Horsley, ed., *Paul and Empire: Religion and Power in Roman Imperial Society* (Harrisburg, Penn.: Trinity Press International, 1997), pp.140-41.

[13]N. T. Wright, *Paul's Gospel and Caesar's Empire*, accessed February 5, 2008, at <www.ctinquiry.org/publications/reflections_volume_2/wright.htm>.

It is important to understand that this application of imperial language and imagery to Jesus was not mere mimicry or analogy but subversive defiance against the emperor. In ancient Middle Eastern monarchical and imperial culture, claiming the attributes and privileges of the king was tantamount to treason. The Jews understood full well the messianic claims of Jesus were claims of kingship. It was after all, the prophesied attribute of the Messiah in the Old Testament that he would be the king who will "set up a kingdom which will never be destroyed, and that kingdom . . . will crush and put an end to all  these kingdoms, but it will itself endure forever" (Dan 2:44). This might be akin to a small cult of people in America going around claiming that their cult leader is president of the United States *and* the Supreme Court, and will ultimately crush America and its leaders. Of course, Jesus—the stone "cut without hands" (Dan 2:44-45)—*did* crush the Roman Empire, yet not overnight like the Jews expected.[14] The first-century Jews understood Jesus to be clearly defying the emperor's claim to universal power and authority when they said of the Christians, "They all act contrary to the decrees of Caesar, saying there is another king, Jesus" (Acts 17:7). And when the chief priests called for Christ's crucifixion, they repeated their submission to Roman rule with the oath, "We have no king but Caesar" (Jn 19:15). To call Christ a higher king than Caesar, let alone another king, was treason to the imperial decree, an action that called for crucifixion.

The gospel message of the cross of Christ became an image of re-

---

[14]The Pauline concept of this "now and not yet" kingdom is that Christ's death and resurrection was the inauguration of this conquering kingdom in its initial breaking of the powers of darkness (Col 2:14-15). But the outworking of this initial beachhead of victory would take time through history, step by step, conquered foe by conquered foe, until the end when Christ returns and hands the kingdom over to the Father (1 Cor 15:22-28). This explains Hebrews' ironic pronouncement that "all things are in subjection under his feet . . . but now we do not yet see all things subjected to him" (Heb 2:8).

verse propaganda. In the Roman Empire, crucifixion was an effective image displaying the might of imperial justice and deterrence. We must not forget that what is to us a religious spiritual symbol was to Roman subjects an image of brutality and terror. So it would be truly "foolish" at that time to speak of crucifixion in terms of any kind of victory. It would be like saying someone executed on the electric chair was victorious. But New Testament writers like Paul turned the imagery against itself by declaring the cross an act of triumph over rulers and authorities (Col 2:15).[15]

Thus, in 1 Corinthians, Christ's resurrection from the dead concludes in his imperial reign from heaven in the present day, putting his enemies one by one "under his feet," much like the colonizing of Rome (1 Cor 15:25) until he "comes" to "abolish all rule and authority and power," a subversive attack on the absolute power of Rome, what Paul called earlier "the rulers of this age" (1 Cor 2:8). Even Paul's description in Ephesians of spiritual armor against the "rulers, powers and world forces of this darkness" is the imagery of an imperial army (Eph 6:12-17). As Neil Elliott concludes, "it is the resurrection of Christ the crucified that reveals the imminent defeat of the Powers, pointing forward to the final triumph of God."[16] The "coming" (Greek: *parousia*) of Christ referred to five times in 1 Thessalonians,[17] and our "meeting" (*apantesis*) of him with trumpets and glorious fanfare (1 Thess 4:16-17) is a reflection of the imperial arrival of Caesar to a Roman city, where the inhabitants come out to meet him in honor.[18]

---

[15]Imperial order was very hierarchical, stressing rulers and authorities on all levels. Neil Elliott, "The Anti-Imperial Message of the Cross," in Horsley, ed., *Paul and Empire, pp. 167-83.

[16]Ibid., p. 181.

[17]See 1 Thess 1:10; 2:19; 3:13; 4:15; 5:23.

[18]Helmut Koester, "Imperial Ideology and Paul's Eschatology in 1 Thessalonians," in Horsley,

Ironically, the entry into the city gates by the Roman Emperor is deliberately subverted in Christ's entry into Jerusalem on a donkey (Mt 21:1-5). The imperial visit, also referred to as Caesar's "adventus," included a parade of armed forces, followed by a golden chariot or throne carrying the emperor, crowned and carrying a palm branch. The citizens would shout salutations in awe of his godlike stature and salvific powers.[19] In the Gospel version, Jesus arrives amid *Hosannas* ("Save, we pray") and palm branches. But his humble status, "gentle, and mounted on a donkey, even a colt, the foal of a beast of burden," subversively undermines worldly military

Christ's Entry into Jerusalem,
by Albrecht Dürer

or political power and glory. In fact, God's contempt for this ironic contrast is best described as mockery (Ps 2:1-9, esp. v. 4).

The early Christians picked up this technique of irony used in the Gospels and implemented it into their art in order to further their subversion of the Roman Empire and its pantheon of gods. Christian art from as early as A.D. 300 depicts Christ in poses that resemble the emperor or Roman deities as depicted on coinage and other Roman art.

---

ed., *Paul and Empire,* pp. 158-66. See Josephus *Antiquities* 11.327ff. for a primary source of this imperial *parousia* and *apantesis.*
[19]Thomas F. Mathews, *The Clash of the Gods: A Reinterpretation of Early Christian Art* (Princeton, N.J.: Princeton University Press, 1993, 1995), pp. 24-27.

Christ is often pictured as enthroned among his apostles like a deity in a pantheon and the emperor on his throne;[20] complete with gold paint and halos, Roman images used for deity.[21] Compositions are often symmetrical and frontal in display, a likeness of imperial art and glory;[22] funerary tables of the mighty Hercules were replaced with funerary tables of the gentle Good Shepherd;[23] a predominance of art illustrating Christ's miracles, more common than any other images in this time period, indicated a "war of images" with the ineffectual pagan magic so common in the ancient world.[24] Early Christian art was subversive of Roman Empire and Roman magic religion.

Yet another way in which the New Testament writers may have subverted the prevailing Imperial culture is in the notion of Christian assemblies or local churches. The Greek word for "church" in the New Testament is *ekklēsia*. But translating the word this way misses an im-

[20]Ibid., pp. 3-5, 107-8.
[21]Ibid., p. 101.
[22]Ibid., p. 14.
[23]Ibid., p. 8.
[24]Ibid., pp. 59, 65-67.

portant context for the first-century Christians. The "primary meaning of *ekklēsia* in the Greek-speaking eastern Roman empire was the citizen 'assembly' of the Greek polis,"[25] a term which had evolved from the Greek idea of local democratic cities ruled by kings[26] into the Roman idea of local communities centered around patron gods festivals and customs under the supreme authority of Caesar. Diana, for example, was the patron goddess of Ephesus around whom the economic, political and religious cult thrived (Acts 19:23-41). The power of Rome prospered in allowing city-states their local deities and customs, so long as they rendered unto Caesar worship as the supreme head over all. So the apostolic emphasis on the Christian *ekklēsia* as an alternative community apart from the local deities and *without* worship of Caesar was a decided subversion of the Roman imperial order of assemblies. This alternative Christian community awaiting the apocalyptic overthrow of imperial hegemony ultimately disturbed the *pax Romana*, resulting in the tribulation and persecution of Christians under Emperor Nero, during which Christians were accused of being "haters of the human race" by imperial inquisitors.[27] Of course, the Jews engaged in persecution of the Christians as well for their subversive defiance of their own traditions.[28] The notion of Christian *ekklēsia* ("assembly") had its primary origins in the ancient Hebrew Old Testament concept of the "assembly of the LORD" (1 Chron 28:8). The synagogue was the basic local unit of Jewish cult that met on the Sabbath, so the Jewish Christians having their own synagogue on Sunday in celebration of Messiah's resurrection was a subversive alteration of Jewish culture (Mk 16:9; Acts 20:7). So in a way, Christian *ekklēsia* was subver-

---

[25]Horsley, *Paul and Empire,* pp. 208-9.

[26]"Polis," accessed at Wikipedia, February 5, 2008, at <http://en.wikipedia.org/wiki/Polis>.

[27]Kenneth L. Gentry Jr., *The Beast of Revelation* (Powder Springs, Ga.: American Vision, 2002), p. 51. Gentry is referring to the primary source of Roman historica, Tacitus, in his *Annals* 1544.

[28]John 20:19; Acts 8:1-3; Mark 7:5.

sive not only of Rome but also of Jerusalem. Which leads us to the next point.

SUBVERSION OF JEWISH CULTURE

It is important to remember that the Gospels are not merely subversive of pagan imagery and culture, they are first and foremost subversive of ancient Jewish culture itself! The Jewish expectation of a conquering military messiah is not only reflected in the Dead Sea Scrolls of the Qumran community[29] and the manifold revolutionary sects of the first century[30] but also in the hostile reaction of the Jews toward Jesus' claim to be Messiah. Although Messiah as suffering servant and *spiritual* victor is not a

Christ Reveals Himself to John, by Julius Schnorr von Carolsfeld

[29]See for instance, Theodor H. Gaster, trans., *The Triumph of God: Descriptions of the Final Age,* in *The Dead Sea Scriptures,* 3rd ed. (New York: Doubleday, 1976), pp. 383-428.
[30]Flavius Josephus, *The Wars of the Jews,* in *The Works of Josephus* (Peabody, Mass.: Hendrickson, 1987, 1992).

redefinition of the Old Testament prophecies (Is 53), it is certainly under-mining of the prevalent expectations of first-century Jews who had *mis-understood* the Scriptures and were looking for worldly deliverance from the Romans as God's promised victory.

N. T. Wright has pointed out that the narrative of Luke reflects not only a Hellenistic biographic approach (thus casting it in terms understood by his pagan readers) but also a retelling of the Davidic story of kingship.[31] Both David's and Jesus' stories are outlined with a prior herald's birth (Samuel and John the Baptizer), a mother's song of praise and gratitude, judgment on Israel for rejection of God's word, the life of an outcast with a motley crew of followers in the desert, an anointing of kingship by the herald, a Spirit anointing, a declaration of sonship,[32] a battle with a monster in the desert, further wandering in the desert, and a triumphal arrival in Jerusalem.[33] Jesus' life was retold as a Davidic story—the Son of David to sit on his throne (Lk 1:32)—to subvert the Jewish expectation of a revolutionary political military ruler of violence with a Messiah of suffering and a kingdom of spirit without physical weapons.

Luke is not the only one to subvert with his Gospel. Matthew subverts the Jewish exile and return story of Israel, and retells it as believers in Jesus forming the true descendants of Abraham, Isaac and Jacob. Jesus is the "Joshua" that brings the Jews into the land of blessings and curses promised in Deuteronomy 30:15-20.[34]

Mark's Gospel subverts the apocalyptic unveiling of mysteries and se-

---

[31]"I will raise up your descendant after you, who will come forth from you, and I will estab-lish his kingdom. He shall build a house for My name, and I will establish the throne of his kingdom forever. I will be a father to him and he will be a son to Me" (2 Sam 7:12-14); "And so, because he was a prophet, and knew that God had sworn to him with an oath to seat one of his descendants upon his throne" (Acts 2:30).

[32]"I will be a father to him and he will be a son to Me" (2 Sam 7:14); "And a voice came out of heaven, 'You are My beloved Son, in You I am well-pleased'" (Lk 3:22).

[33]N. T. Wright, *The New Testament and the People of God* (Minneapolis: Fortress, 1992), pp. 378-83.

[34]Ibid., p. 388.

crets of the kingdom of God by reversing the Jewish expectations of justice. As Wright explains, in Mark's subversion,

> The coming of the kingdom does not mean the great vindication of Jerusalem, the glorification of the Temple, the real return from exile envisaged by the prophets and their faithful readers. It means rather, the desolation of Jerusalem, the destruction of the Temple, and the vindication of Jesus and his people.[35]

The Gospel of John uses language that seems to subvert Hellenistic mystery religion. But conservative scholars have recently suggested that the opening of John's Gospel about the Logos (indeed the whole of the Gospel) reflects a subversion of "wisdom" that is more Hebraic than Hellenistic.[36] And that Hebraic concept is reflected not only in Genesis, but in the apocryphal books and Dead Sea Scrolls leading up to the New Testament:[37]

> Wisdom will praise herself, and will glory in the midst of her people. In the assembly of the Most High she will open her mouth, and in the presence of his host she will glory. . . . Then the Creator of all things gave me a commandment, and the one who created me assigned a place for my tent. And he said, "Make your dwelling in Jacob, and in Israel receive your inheritance." From eternity, in the beginning, he created me, and for eternity I shall not cease to exist. . . . All this is the book of the covenant of the Most High God, the law which Moses commanded us as an inheritance for the congregations of Jacob. (*Ben Sirach* 24:1-24)

In this Hebrew scroll we see wisdom with God in the beginning, just as

[35]Ibid., p. 395.
[36]Ibid., pp. 410-17.
[37]James H. Charlesworth, ed., *John and the Dead Sea Scrolls* (New York: Crossroad, 1991). C. K. Barrett, *The Gospel According to St. John: An Introduction with Commentary and Notes on the Greek Text,* 2nd ed. (Philadelphia: Westminster Press, 1978).

Logos was with God in the beginning in John. Wisdom is given a tent, just like Jesus "pitched his tent" in John 1:14. Wisdom has glory just as Jesus has glory (Jn 1:14). The law comes through Moses in *Ben Sirach*, just as it is affirmed in John 1:17, but expanded to add grace and truth being realized through Jesus Christ. The parallels are strong, as they are with Hellenism, reflecting perhaps more accurately that the kind of language John used was universal within the culture, concepts utilized by most religious and cultural communities of the era for their own purposes.

Everyone used a similar vocabulary of light and darkness, wisdom and word, life and death, spirit and flesh, and simply subverted those terms within their own thought forms.[38]

Jesus himself was a master subversive storyteller who entered the Jewish history of hope, and retold that story of exodus, exile and return in terms that turned the Jewish expectations upside down. His parables are strong indictments against the "chosen people" who reject their own messiah and instead receive judgment upon themselves, while the "rejected ones" (Gentiles, Samaritans, tax collectors, prostitutes and other sinners) enter into the kingdom (Mt 21:31-32). The parables of the vineyard (Mt 21:33-43), the tree barren of fruit (Lk 13:6-9), the unfaithful servant (Mt 24:45-51), the prodigal son (Lk 15), the Pharisee and tax collector (Lk 18:9-14), the ten virgins (Mt 25:1-13), the hidden talents (Mt 25:14-30), the sheep and the goats (Mt 25:31-46) and the wedding feast (Mt 22:1-14; 8:11-12) are all subversive stories of images that illustrate the false assumption of the Jewish people as righteous before God.

Jesus' healings of the blind, deaf and dumb, lepers, cripples, the possessed, Gentiles, Samaritans and other ritually "unclean" persons bore witness to "the inclusion within the people of YHWH of those who had for-

---

[38]D. A. Carson, *The Gospel According to John* (Grand Rapids: Eerdmans, 1991), pp. 59-60.

Sermon on the Mount, by Julius Schnorr von Carolsfeld

merly been outside,"[39] a reconstitution of the people of God by gathering the outcast into God's new community, the kingdom of heaven. His parables of God seeking and saving the lost like a woman for a coin or a shepherd after a lost sheep or the prodigal son (Lk 15) were implicit defiance of the Jewish community's rejection of the "other" as embodied in the gentiles or "sinners."

Wright points out that Jesus' parables were not merely tales of "timeless dogma or ethics" but rather an entire retelling of the story of Israel with a new agenda much in the same way as someone might undermine the received history of a country's heroic growth of freedom by retelling it in terms of exploitation and power. The Olivet Discourse in Matthew 23—24 and Luke 21, as well as the book of Revelation, are prophecies of judgment upon first-century Israel for rejecting the Messiah. The destruc-

---

[39]N. T. Wright, *Jesus and the Victory of God* (Minneapolis: Fortress, 1996), p. 192.

tion of Jerusalem and the Temple that occurred in A.D. 70 is then described as a result of such rejection.[40] As Jesus clearly states to his hearers of the first-century generation:

Herod's Temple in Jerusalem

"Jerusalem, Jerusalem, who kills the prophets and stones those who are sent to her! How often I wanted to gather your children together, the way a hen gathers her chicks under her wings, and you were unwilling. Behold, your house is being left to you desolate!" . . . Jesus came out from the temple and was going away when His disciples came up to point out the temple buildings to Him. And He said to them, "Do you not see all these things? Truly I say to you, not one stone here will be left upon another, which will not be torn down." (Mt 23:37—24:2)

Perhaps Jesus' most indicting subversion of Israel is his parable of the vineyard in Matthew 21, where he likens Israel's rejection of his Messiahship to the rejection and killing of a vineyard owner's son, resulting in the destruction of those vine-growers and the renting out of the vineyard to others. This parable, a retelling of Isaiah's similar parable (Is 5), ends with the ultimate subversion from Jesus' own lips, "Therefore I say to you, the kingdom of God will be taken away from you and given to a people, producing the fruit of it" (Mt 21:43).

In all these parables and images, this presumption of Jewish righteous standing is turned on its head by God who rejects such arrogance in favor

---

[40] I highly recommend the following books for more information on the Olivet Discourse prophecies: Gary DeMar, *Last Day Madness: Obsession of the Modern Church* (Atlanta: American Vision, 1997), Kenneth L. Gentry Jr., *The Beast of Revelation* (Powder Springs, Ga.: American Vision, 2002) and the novel series *The Last Disciple* by Hank Hanegraaff and Sigmund Brouwer (Wheaton, Ill.: Tyndale House, 2004-2007).

of the "outcast," the repentant sinner. Wright concludes, "This ties in, of course, with the use of apocalyptic, which (as we now know) is at least in part to be understood as the literature of subversion, of the cryptic undermining of a dominant and powerful worldview, and the encouraging and supporting of a revolutionary one."[41] God scandalously chooses the "unchosen" to be his people—much to the shock and chagrin of those who considered themselves chosen through family birth:

> As He says also in Hosea, "I will call those who were not My people, 'My people,' And her who was not beloved, 'beloved.'" "And it shall be that in the place where it was said to them, 'you are not My people,' There they shall be called sons of the living God." (Rom 9:25-26)

As the Temple served as a metaphor for the covenant along with the language of creation of the universe, so its destruction was described in the metaphoric image of the end of the universe. Now we see in the New Testament the subversion of Temple imagery. Following Jesus, the apostle Peter redefines a host of Old Testament imagery in terms of New Testament covenant, along the way describing the body of Christ as the rebuilt temple:

> And coming to Him as to a living stone which has been rejected by men, but is choice and precious in the sight of God, you [Christians] also, as living stones, are being built up as a spiritual house for a holy priesthood, to offer up spiritual sacrifices acceptable to God through Jesus Christ. (1 Pet 2:4-5)

Peter then images Jesus as that cornerstone of the new Temple:

> For this is contained in Scripture: "Behold, I lay in Zion a choice stone, a precious corner stone, And he who believes in Him will not

---

[41]Wright, *Jesus and the Victory of God*, p. 179.

be disappointed." This precious value, then, is for you who believe. (1 Pet 2:6-7)

Lastly, Peter subverts the Old Testament language used of ethnic Jews ("chosen people," "holy nation," royal priesthood") and applies that terminology to all believers in Jesus:

> But you are a chosen race, a royal priesthood, a holy nation, a people for God's own possession, so that you may proclaim the excellencies of Him who has called you out of darkness into His marvelous light; for you once were not a people, but now you are the people of God; you had not received mercy, but now you have received mercy. (1 Pet 2:9-10)

Descent of the Holy Ghost,
by Julius Schnorr von Carolsfeld

Christianity, though it was the intended messianic fulfillment of the Old Covenant promises, was nevertheless a subversion of a first-century Jewish worldview that had strayed from the Scriptures into rabbinic distortion, thereby missing the very Messiah they looked for. With this radical subversion of Jewish expectations and the transformation of the entire symbolic system of Temple, Torah, blood and soil, into Jesus and his followers, it is no wonder the apostles of that subversive message were all martyred, save one.[42]

RECENT CHRISTIAN HEROES OF SUBVERSION

Rather than separating himself into the Christian enclave of "holy subculture," Paul and the other biblical writers interacted redemptively with their Jewish and pagan surroundings. They assimilated Jewish and pagan imagery into a Christian worldview and redefined it. They found points of connection and truth, and affirmed them. They also pointed out where Christianity was distinct and antithetical. But they interacted with the culture. They did not avoid it. So Christians today should expose themselves to and even participate in the music, movies and television of today with an eye toward the truth—*within* the media as well as the truth without it.

An excellent example of Christian appropriation of pagan mythology and images are the famous Christian fantasy writers C. S. Lewis and J. R. R. Tolkien. Their love of pagan Nordic mythology united them in their early club, The Coal Biters. Later, this influence showed up in their writing, such as Tolkien's Lord of the Rings trilogy and Lewis's seven-volume Chronicles of Narnia. Tolkien's stories abound with the mythical Norse characters of wizards, dwarves, elves, giants, trolls and others.[43] Lewis's stories are saturated with beasts from assorted pagan mythologies. *The Lion, the Witch, and the Wardrobe* alone contains the phoenix of Egyptian origin; Bacchus, the Roman god of wine; minotaurs, fauns, centaurs, unicorns, and gryphons from Greco-Roman paganism. And then there are the witches, as well as animistic tree nymphs, wood nymphs and water nymphs.

---

[42]N. T. Wright, *The New Testament and the People of God* (Minneapolis: Fortress, 1992), pp. 450-51.

[43]See Andy Orchard, *Cassell's Dictionary of Norse Myth and Legend* (London: Cassell, 2002).

For years I struggled with the notion of using such fantasy characters of pagan origin in Christian art. The strongest example of this is the use of witches. I labored over the use of witches in non-Christian stories like the Harry Potter series as opposed to the use of such creatures of magic in the Christian fantasies of Lewis and Tolkien. On the one hand, Harry Potter seems to "normalize" witchcraft and support the possibility of good and bad witches. Contrarily, the Bible condemns all forms of witchcraft as evil (Deut. 18:9-14). There is no such thing as good or evil witches in the Bible. There is only one kind of witchcraft and that is the evil kind.

And yet how different are Lewis and Tolkien's witches or for that matter, their "magic"? Yes, Lewis's White Witch is evil, which is consistent with Scripture, but the other mythological creatures, good and evil, are equally as pagan (wizards, satyrs, fairies, and centaurs). And Tolkien's good and bad wizards are simply male witches. So there is not all that much difference in that sense between Potter and Narnia or Middle Earth.[44]

Reflecting on biblical passages that not only referenced pagan myths and images but used them in the service of Christianity helped me to realize that images that originate in pagan beliefs such as animism can be put to good Christian use if they are used imaginatively. This is exactly what the godly Jotham did in the Bible when he confronted Judah with a parable of talking trees that seek a king and end up convincing a bramble bush to rule over them (Judg 9:7-15). Throughout Scripture we read of riv-

---

[44]A bigger problem, as I see it, with Harry Potter is not so much that author J. K. Rowling classifies good and bad witches but that some of the Potter stories tend to justify the pragmatic morality of situational ethics. Lying, disobedience to authority and breaking rules are justified in the first book when they result in good being accomplished. This "ends justifying the means" is unbiblical and detrimental to the spiritual well-being of the children who absorb it (Rom 3:8; 1 Cor 15:33). On the other hand, there are also strong themes of loyalty, friendship, courage and other Christian values in the Potter series, which makes it a mixture of good and bad.

ers and trees clapping their hands in praise of God and mountains singing songs of joy (Is 55:12; Ps 98:8) or having envy (Ps 68:16) as if these inanimate objects had souls and could relate to God. Jesus used talking sheep and goats as an allegory of the final judgment (Mt 25:36-41). And Balaam's donkey argued with her master over his failure to trust his beast of burden's spiritual insight (Num 22:28-30). The many-headed beast of Revelation 13:5-6 is a foul-mouthed monstrosity, while the flying talking eagle of Revelation 8:13 is a righteous prophet. Even the holy union of Christ with the church is represented as a woman (the bride) marrying an animal (the Lamb) in Revelation 19:6-9. These are all scriptural examples of animism used metaphorically in the service of God.

In like manner, Lewis and Tolkien seem to use magic and witchcraft more as a metaphor for something else than as a sign of real-world gnos-

tic manipulation of reality. Lewis's "deep magic" is an allegorical metaphor for the Law of God and the order he has ordained for reality. The pagan mythological characters in the Chronicles of Narnia are simply various images reflecting man's misguided imaginative perceptions of God—an acknowledgment of the universal reality created by God and distorted by the Fall.

Tolkien's entire Middle Earth mythology of magic was a metaphor for the loss of the sacred in modernity. He saw Enlightenment scientific rationalism and its spawn, the Industrial Revolution, as the killer of the spiritual side of man.[45] This was the result not of modernist environmentalism but of his Roman Catholic medieval unity of knowledge and life before God. Tolkien's method is similarly employed in the horror genre in art, novels and films.

[45]The Rough Guide to the Lord of the Rings (Strand, U.K.: Penguin, 2003), pp. 277-78.

Horror communicates a very clear picture of the world as containing real evil. In this era of postmodern relative morality where people actually try to justify atrocities by appealing to moral equivalency (ie: "one man's terrorist is another man's freedom fighter"), this elementary notion of good and evil is rather profound. In horror, one man's serial killer is really a serial killer and his evil is undeniably without moral equivalency. Christian film-

maker Scott Derrickson's *The Exorcism of Emily Rose* uses the horror genre to communicate a strong spiritual reality to a modernist world of positiv-

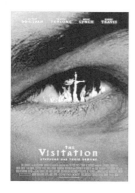

istic science. My own film adaptation of Frank Peretti's Christian horror novel *The Visitation* sought to use demonic deception as a corollary to a lack of true understanding of Christ. A look at the origins of modern horror from the Romantic period *(Frankenstein, Dracula, Dr. Jekyll and Mr. Hyde)* reveals a rather Christian influence in revealing the negative ramifications of man's hubris and immorality.[46]

SUBVERTING CHRISTIANITY

Sadly, one of the most powerful recent examples of subversion was in fact a non-Christian movie trilogy, *The Matrix*, that subverted Christian themes. The cinematic equivalent of Friedrich Nietzsche's book *Thus Spake Zarathustra* or Jean Baudrillard's *Simulacra and Simulation*, *The Matrix* trilogy runs multiple religious images—mostly from Christianity—through a Nietzschean interpretation that deconstructs all these faiths

---

[46]E. Michael Jones, *Monsters from the Id: The Rise of Horror in Fiction and Film* (Dallas: Spence Publishing, 2000).

Figure 7.1.

into Gnostic salvation of redemption through self-enlightenment. The series marked a turning point in mainstream society from modernism to postmodernism.

The movies shown in figure 7.1 were all successful popular movies about heroes who in real life were Christians, whose faith influenced their exploits. Yet, every one of these movies either entirely ignored that faith or downplayed it to virtual irrelevancy. Paul Rusesabagina was the man profiled in *Hotel Rwanda;* his Christian faith caused him to reach out and help those who were being slaughtered in the 1990s Rwandan genocide. But you would never know that because the filmmakers did not depict his faith.

The protagonist of *The Pursuit of Happyness,* Chris Gardner, was helped by the values of his faith, such as the Protestant work ethic, that helped him overcome his poverty. But you would never know that because filmmakers successfully hid his faith.

The film *Becoming Jane* fictionalizes Jane Austen's life. Along the way it eliminates her Christian faith, depicting her as a humanistic protofeminist romantic instead.

The real Anna Leonowens who married the King of Siam was a Christian missionary whose faith informed her values. But you wouldn't know that because her faith was non-existent in *Anna and the King.*

Two movies about Pocahontas—*The New World* and *Pocahontas*—deliberately ignore the woman's conversion to Christianity, and even go so far as to romanticize the Native American animism that she rejected.

In the second half of his life, after his encounter with God in a cave, Johnny Cash was all about Jesus. But you wouldn't know that from *Walk the Line,* because this movie stops chronologically before the most profound redemption and character arc takes place. The movie portrays Cash being saved by June Carter, rather than by Jesus Christ.

In real life, the protagonist that *Hardball* was based on, Daniel Coyle, brought redemption to inner-city kids through his faith in Jesus Christ. But you wouldn't know that because the movie depicted him as a profane, foul-mouthed jerk who becomes a humanistic humanitarian.

The hero that the film *The Patriot* was based on, Francis Marion, was fueled in his ambition for American independence by his Christianity, a fact almost entirely ignored in the movie, save for a trivial shot of prayer.

Other movies, such as *Inherit the Wind* (1960), *1492* (1992), *Titanic* (1997), *King Arthur* (2005), *Kingdom of Heaven* (2005), *Children of Men* (2006), and *Beowulf* (2007) are successful movies that took the Christian themes of the original material and twisted them into anti-Christian themes, thus in effect raping the faith of the original authors. These movies are examples of how powerful subversion can be. In essence, these Christian stories have been captured and retold through paradigms of "good works" or the "power of the human spirit" or some other humanistic fiction rather than through the living vital faith of the heroes.

Those who capture the culture not only tell their own stories but reinterpret the stories of their opponents through their own worldview. This is not necessarily dishonest; we all interpret and reinterpret history through our worldviews. Christians should tell their own stories of martyrs or missionaries, but we should not neglect to retell the stories of atheists and humanists like Darwin, Stalin, Marx, Nietzsche and Freud and others through our worldview. Subversion is the nature of storytelling, and storytelling is how anyone wins a culture.

EIGHT

What Art Would Jesus Do?

The church of Jesus Christ has had a troubled relationship with the arts throughout history. Perhaps one of the reasons why lies in the very nature of creativity, which is driven to discover new and original ways of communicating or seeing things.

This search for newness often results in new styles of art that challenge the status quo with revolutionary implications on the way we see the world. While many Christians today find Impressionism an acceptable painting style, they rarely realize that it was originally received with derision, due to its origins in the philosophy of naturalism.[1] This belief—that there is no spiritual reality and everything is reducible to sense impressions—was taken to its logical conclusion: reality itself is merely reflections of light in our eyes.

From rock music to abstract expressionism to horror movies,

---

[1]H. R. Rookmaaker, *Modern Art and the Death of a Culture* (Downers Grove, Ill.: InterVarsity Press, 1971), pp. 82-87.

Christians have often reacted with hostility to
the surface elements of artistic styles in
music, painting, theater, film, and literature rather than understanding the
worldview below the surface. Because
abstract expressionists like Jackson Pol-
lock painted chaotically, all abstract expression becomes godless. Because some hor-
ror movies exploit fear and violence, all scary movies become
"demonic."

Such reactionism is biblically unwarranted. A survey of the
styles of art and literature in the Bible unveils a plethora of genres,
including abstract art and horror, that have been used for both
evil and good in the history of art. What makes the art evil or
good is not the style but the worldview that
the style is servicing. Abstraction
may appear ugly to some people,
but even so, ugliness is part of the biblical
painting of the world in the Fall. Representational or realistic art can be used to ex-
press the beauty of creation or a godless philosophy of naturalism.
Horror can be used to exploit fear and sexuality or to prove the
real existence of evil to a world that believes in relativism.[2]

RULES OF BEAUTY

Christians who are influenced by modernity are conditioned to
seek for absolute rules of good and bad art. Rap isn't real music,
abstract expressionism isn't real painting, and so on. The problem
with this categorizing agenda is that, while there may be some

---

[2]See my book *Hollywood Worldviews* for a discussion of how worldviews are communicated through film.

rules regarding the nature of how art affects the viewer, rules for art that are traditionally recognized in conservative circles are too often unbiblical. When observed in the light of Scripture, these absolutes dissolve into a sea of a thousand biblical qualifications. Let's take a closer look at some of these rules to see how absolute and unbiblical they really are.

REALISM OVER NONREALISM

Realistic art is often elevated in Christian circles above other artistic styles. There is a marked tendency to consider fantasy, myth, abstraction, symbolism and other non-representational styles as less legitimate than realism or representational art. The more literal, the better; the more obvious the better; the more "like real-life" the better. This is often linked to a desire for "literalism" in interpreting the Bible. Some say a realistic story meets a person where they are; a literal picture of reality is more easily understood than symbol; representations of things in the world are safer than flights of fantasy.

Unfortunately these well-meaning Christians do not realize that this elevation of realism springs from the naturalistic scientific claim that the empirical world—what we see with our senses—is all there is. It hides the central conceit of modernity that reality can be known objectively and without prejudice or bias by our mere observation. In this context, realism is anything but real. It is the claim that the way things appear is the way they really are, that there is no underlying reality.

Taken this way, realism becomes a façade for nihilism, the belief that there is no meaning, purpose or value to life. There is just "what happens," and "that's reality, baby." Realism becomes a life lived in the Matrix. Christianity is realistic in that it portrays the way things really are, but not often in a realistic style. Vast metaphors, symbols, analogies and poetry are used to describe the spiritual or metaphysical reality beneath the outward appearance of human experience. I know a lot of nice people who are not Christians and don't seem bad as human beings. They do good, they seem to be free and open to truth, and some of them are even well-adjusted and fulfilled. But is this reality? Like Morpheus explaining to Neo, so Jesus and the apostles unveil an apocalyptic quite different from the way things appear: no one is ultimately good (Lk 18:19); all unbelievers are rebels against God (Rom 3:9-12), slaves to their sin (Jn 8:34), blind (2 Cor 4:4), spiritually dead (Eph 2:1) and without hope (Eph 2:12). Realism is not the full picture.

HARMONY OVER DISHARMONY

Often religious folk have the belief that songs that do not have a harmonious order, paintings that are messy and disturbingly imbalanced, and movies that are "dark and negative" reflect an ungodly viewpoint in the artist or work. "Family-friendly" arts and entertainment that stress harmony or order and positivity are to be preferred over those showing disharmony or negativity. After all, "God is not a God of confusion, but of peace" (1 Cor 14:33).

To be sure, the Bible is a book that communicates an ultimate harmony and ultimate order for God and the universe. But because it is a fallen world, we are not there yet, so the Bible deals very openly with the disorder around us. The nature of the entire Bible is one of conflict between light and darkness. There are periods of great darkness (Judges), and spiritual apostasy (minor and major prophets). God often gives disturbing visions and images in order to bring back the harmony or order that was lost (Revelation).

Moreover, sometimes harmony can be idolatrous. In the pagan culture of unified harmony and peace under Caesar or Nebuchadnezzar, to stand apart and be out of harmony with the prevailing order would be in fact the godly thing to do. Sometimes art needs to be disturbing and out of order with the times if the times are indeed evil as the Bible says they are (1 Cor 2:6; Col 2:20-21).

LINEARITY OVER NONLINEARITY

Some Christians think that nonlinearity is ungodly in art. They believe that a story out of chronological sequence is irrational and therefore not good. Nonlinearity is an offense to rationalism because it appears to deny the order of reality.

The Bible's overall narrative is linear in its organization: Genesis (beginning), redemptive history (middle), and eschaton (end). But within this overarching order there are cyclical histories (1-2 Kings), multiple perspectives (four Gospels), as well as nonlinear chronology (Isaiah, Jeremiah, Revelation). And the major and minor prophets are certainly not placed in their respective linear chronology within the text. The Scriptures are inherently multiperspectival, being written by kings and slaves, princes and paupers, from God's perspective as well as from the perspective of saints and sinners. The nonlinearity and perspectivalism in the Bible serve a higher, God-directed purpose and ought not be feared.

STYLES OF ART IN THE BIBLE

Francis Schaeffer's classic little book *Art and the Bible* contains a survey of art used in the Bible.[3] In addition to representational art for the tabernacle and temple (Ex 25:18,31), God also commands abstract art (Ex 28:33), symbolic art (Ex 28:15), art as sacrament (Num 21:8) and art for beauty's sake (Ex 28:2). In the Scriptures,

---

[3]Francis Schaeffer, *Art and the Bible* (Downers Grove, Ill.: InterVarsity Press, 1973).

The Vision of the Valley of Dry Bones, by Gustave Doré

there is not merely religious art such as sacred poetry (Psalms), but so-called secular art: friendship poetry (2 Sam 1:19-27), erotic romance novels (Song of Solomon) and civic sculpture (1 Kings 10:18-20). God employs the genres of epic (Exodus), Romance (Ruth and Esther), erotic thriller (Prov 7), horror and fantasy (Dan 7), and absurdist drama (Ecclesiastes). God clearly enjoys loud music, singing (1 Chron 23:5) and dancing (Ps 149:3), as well as their opposites: chanting (Ezek 32:16), silence ("selah" throughout Psalms) and stillness (Ps 4:4).

God had his prophets put on war dramas (Ezek 4:1-3), engage in shocking performance art (Is 20:2-4), tell parables (Mt 13:3), allegories (2 Sam 12:1-7), symbolic fantasies (Judg 9:7-15), zombie stories (Gen 41:19-21) and other monster and sci-fi horror epics (Revelation). Jesus' fictional parables run the gamut of genres with gangster stories (Mt 18:6), macabre horror (Mt 18:8-9), family drama (Lk 15:11-32), thrillers (Mt 18:23-35), courtroom dramas (Lk 18:1-8), revenge stories (Mt 21:33-41), corporate espionage (Lk 16:1-9), animal tales (Mt 25:36-41), tragedies (Mt 24:45-51) and comedies (Lk 15:3-10).

The fact that most of these examples from Scripture are literary styles does not restrict the analogy to literature. Abstraction, realism, symbolism and others exist in all creativity, including music and the visual arts. There are simply so many styles that God has used or approved of that it would be ludicrous to try to condemn any particular style of art simply because godless people are using that style to communicate an aspect of their godless worldview. Scripture often employs these same styles of art that modern Christians bristle at. It is not the form that necessarily makes the art immoral, it is the content.

Each genre or style of art contains a particular angle that can be used in the service of truth or falsehood as well as employed to exploit evil or expose sin biblically. Consider the "family friendly" cartoons of Disney that teach antibiblical values such as disobedience to parents *(The Little Mermaid, Mulan),* Christianity as the enemy of progress *(The Hunchback of Notre Dame, Beauty and the Beast),* evolution *(Dinosaur),* and the lie of the "noble savage" *(Pocohantas, Tarzan).* Even biblical epics can be a twisting of the truth into a lie (the movie *The Last Temptation of Christ,* the novel *The Red Tent,* Salvador Dali's painting *The Last Supper).* Some so-called Christian movies actually teach a modern "love-gospel" that is far more spiritually detrimental than any slasher flick or erotic thriller.[4]

R-RATED BIBLE

Another aspect of style that afflicts Christian decision-making about the arts is the depiction of sin or the dark side of humanity. Many Christians are rightfully concerned about the increasing amounts of sex and violence in the arts, specifically pop music, television and movies. But when they make sweeping condemnations such as "All R-rated movies are sinful or bad" or "Any sexual reference in music is wrong," they are unwittingly fostering an unscriptural worldview that would condemn their own Bibles. I have spoken at Christian colleges that forbid their students from watching R-rated movies. Where they find this rule in the Bible is yet to be revealed, but ironically, there is no simultaneous restriction on reading R-rated literature. Perhaps

---

[4]The movie *Joshua* depicts a priest who refers to the Law of God and admission of sin as a Pharisee. The Christ figure in the film claims God is only about love, not law or judgment of sin. This "love gospel" has its roots in the ancient heresy of Marcionism, the belief that the God of the Old Testament was harsh and judgmental, while in contrast, the God of the New Testament is loving. The dichotomy of love and judgment in God's character is not biblical. In both Old and New Testaments, God is judge, jury (Ps 7:11; Heb 13:4), executioner (Dan 4; Mt 22:1-14), defense attorney (1 Jn 2:1) and kinsman redeemer (Heb 4:15).

this oversight was deliberate in order to allow the students to read and study their R-rated Bibles. Consider the R-rated books of Judges, 1 and 2 Kings and Chronicles, or the erotic poetry of Song of Solomon.[5]

Another irony is that this prohibition against R-rated material precluded students at one school from seeing *The Passion,* one of the most powerful biblical movies in decades, because of its R rating. Some schools made an exception for *The Passion* because it is about redemption through the violence of the cross. What they fail to understand in their double standard is that the same kind of redemption, even substitutionary atonement (which is part and parcel of the gospel), is found in other violent R-rated movies as well, such as *Braveheart, Collateral, Last of the Mohicans, Man on Fire, Return to Paradise, To End All Wars, Schindler's List* and *The Addiction.*

One of the most common anthropomorphic images in Scripture is that of God as lover or husband to his people. Over and over again, in both Old and New Testaments, God refers to Israel, his people, as a bride or wife (e.g., Jer 31:32; Rev 19:17).

Many Christians try to ignore or deny the erotic poetry of the Song of Solomon by reducing it to an allegory of Christ's love for the church. But even if it is an allegory, it still remains *erotic sexual love poetry,* something most churches would never read to their children, and certainly not in Sunday School.

The metaphor of marriage between God and his bride (the

---

[5]In my book *Hollywood Worldviews: Watching Films with Wisdom and Discernment,* I chronicle and exegete Scriptural passages that prove the Bible is explicit about depravity and not at all shy in describing some sins in morbid or even erotic detail. Parental discretion is advised.

people of God) becomes a springboard for God's imagination when he deals with disobedience or spiritual apostasy. God uses many graphic sexual images to describe unfaithful or hypocritical faith. Just a sampling of such explicit metaphors are adultery (Hosea), prostitution (Hosea, Nahum 3), promiscuity (Ezek 16; 23), bestiality (Jer 13:25-27; Ezek 23:20), sex with inanimate objects (Jer 3:1-9; Ezek 16:17), gang rape (Ezek 23:28-29), indecent exposure (Jer 13:25-27; Nahum 3:5), and even the throwing of feces (Nahum 3:6). The Bible is simply not G-rated literature for family-friendly programming.

SARCASM

Another kind of creative expression that is not as readily embraced in some parts of Christendom is sarcasm. Some Christians feel that sarcasm or satire is harsh and unloving—not befitting a Christlike treatment of people. And a cursory look at American culture confirms that concern to a degree. We are drenched in sarcastic humor that often approaches cynical cruelty. Comedians ruthlessly mock everything from the sanctity of sex to the holiness of God. Chic nihilism reigns in music, movies and television. But does all this sophistry preclude a proper use of sarcasm? What is the Christian's responsibility regarding this dark angle on humor? It turns out that an examination of the Bible yields a rather startling revelation: God uses sarcasm and mockery as an important tool of truth-telling.

God is often sarcastic in his humor. And particularly in relation to sin. In response to the foolishness of sinners gathering together, plotting against God and his anointed Son, King David writes, "He who sits in the heavens laughs, The Lord scoffs

at them" (Ps 2:4-5). God scoffs. He mocks the folly of wicked
men (Ps 37:12-13), He mocks nations of sinners who "howl like
dogs," and "belch forth with their mouths" (Ps 59:6-8). Arrogant rebels deserve to be mocked when comparing them to the
glory of God.

But God does not reserve his acerbic wit for the reprobate
alone. He also employs it against his own regenerate children
when they get out of line. When Job's sincere desire to accept the
deep ways of God turns into a questioning demand to account for
alleged injustice, God responds with eighty-plus sarcastic questions meant to humiliate Job in his hubris. And God prefaces
those questions by mockingly saying, "I will ask
you, and you instruct Me!" (Job 38:3). As if
God has anything to learn from the
brightest star of human intelligence. As if
God is obligated to give an account of his
ways to man (Job 33:13). Questioning God
deserves to be scorned, especially when it is
engaged in by a believer who ought to know better.

Sarcasm is not below God's character, and neither is
it below his people's character. The same laughing derision that
God himself employs toward the wicked is also played out dramatically through God's appointed mockers—I mean messengers.

ELIJAH

When Elijah engages the false prophets of Baal on Mount Carmel
in 1 Kings 18, both he and the enemy prophets place cut-up oxen
on an altar of wood without fire. The challenge: Each will call
upon their own God. And whichever God answers with fire from
heaven upon the altar, he is God.

The Baal prophets call and call and cut themselves like a bunch of nihilistic idiots. But surprise, no fire from heaven. Elijah responds with dripping sarcasm that can only come from the mouth of an anointed servant of God:

> Elijah mocked them and said, "Call out with a loud voice, for he is a god; either he is occupied or gone aside [to the toilet], or is on a journey, or perhaps he is asleep and needs to be awakened." (1 Kings 18:27)

Yahweh, of course, responds with fire from heaven. So the ridicule is clear. A god who is finite and who needs to travel or go the bathroom or sleep is no god at all but a figment of men's idolatrous imaginations. And that is truly a laughing sight worthy of the highest scorn. Dennis Miller, eat your heart out.[6]

ISAIAH

In Isaiah 44 the prophet mocks those who worship idols made of the same wood used for common household tasks. One can hear the sarcasm bellowing in the words put into the idolater's mouth by Isaiah:

> "Aha! I am warm, I have seen the fire." But the rest of it he makes into a god, his graven image. He falls down before it and worships; he also prays to it and says, "Deliver me, for you are my god." (Is 44:16-17)

And atheists think they have a corner on mocking religion.

---

[6]Dennis Miller is a comedian, formerly of *Saturday Night Live,* who earned his reputation for quick, sophisticated sarcastic humor.

God has the longest-running gag about religion
yet—false religion, that is.

PAUL

In 2 Corinthians Paul lays it on heavy
with his own children in the faith. He
sarcastically chides the Corinthians for
their ignorant and foolish acceptance of
false apostles, whom he mockingly calls
"super-apostles":

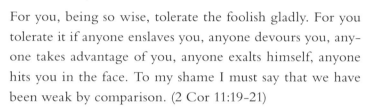

> For you, being so wise, tolerate the foolish gladly. For you
> tolerate it if anyone enslaves you, anyone devours you, any-
> one takes advantage of you, anyone exalts himself, anyone
> hits you in the face. To my shame I must say that we have
> been weak by comparison. (2 Cor 11:19-21)

He calls them "wise" when they obviously are not. He inti-
mates that it is sheer stupidity on the Corinthians' part for failing
to recognize Satan's minions even when they're outright slapping
them in the face (2 Cor 11:13-14)!

Paul concludes by asking them to forgive him for *not*
being a financial burden to them (2 Cor 12:13), as if money-
grubbing is the sign of a true
apostle and preaching for free
was not. This is mockery par-
excellence. Here is some material
for an ancient version of *Late Night
with the Apostle Paul.*

JESUS

But what about Jesus? The man of love and kindness—surely he never used sarcasm or mockery to get a point across.

As the prophet Micaiah would say, go ahead and believe what you want. But here's the truth: Jesus mocked.

In Luke 13:32, for example, Jesus called King Herod a "fox." In ancient Jewish literature, the image of a fox was not only used as a derogatory metaphor for lowly cunning, but more particularly was a reference to people who were of little importance. The fox was a political nuisance who, like the jackal, would scavenge off the kill of a lion (imagery for truly powerful people) and try to dodge the consequences.[7] By using the image of a fox for Herod, Jesus is insulting him in the same way we might today insultingly refer to politicians as "publicity hounds," "weasels," or "sleazebags."

But that's not all. By using the feminine form of the word Jesus is actually calling Herod a "vixen," a female fox, insinuating he was dominated by his unlawful wife Herodias.[8]

THE PUNCHLINE

Of course, these biblical examples do not justify *all* sarcasm. We may not receive actual visions or direct words from God like they did, but we can draw on the principles found in their behavior and act accordingly. For example, we might draw the principle that satire may be appropriate when applied to public sins or evil done by men who openly defy God's law (Lk 13:32; 1 Kings 18:27) but not necessarily to the private sins of individuals with whom we have personal relationships (Mt 18:15). It may be appropriate to ridicule false religions and idolaters for their foolish-

[7]"Animals: Fox or Jackal," in *The Dictionary of Biblical Imagery*, ed. Leland Ryken, James C. Wilhoit and Tremper Longman III (Downers Grove, Ill.: InterVarsity Press, 1998), p. 30.
[8]Greg Bahnsen, *Theonomy in Christian Ethics* (Phillipsburg, N.J.: Presbyterian and Reformed, 1984), pp. 391-92.

Elijah Slaying the Priests of Baal, by Julius Schnorr von Carolsfeld

ness (Is 44:16-17), but not necessarily the moral failures of otherwise godly men (Gal 6:1). Condemning hypocrisy is biblical (Mt 23:13-29), hypocritical condemnation is sinful (Mt 7:1-5). We should degrade false teachers—even by name—in scathing terms (2 Tim 2:17-18) but we should be patient and kind with merely errant or misguided teachers (Phil 1:15-18). We may even chide the body of Christ if it has become hardened of heart, dense-headed or easily fooled, but only with a humble heart and redeeming motives (2 Cor 11). And of course, it is never appropriate to make jabs at God or his word, unless one is begging to be cursed (Job 40).

The danger of using sarcasm notwithstanding, it is certainly one of the most potent tools to make a moral point and expose sin, lies and hypocrisy with an edge of humor. The essence of comedy is precisely that we laugh at our faults and frailties, and yes, even at our sins, which elevates the excellent and the virtuous as superior. Sarcasm reinforces the values we believe in by showing the absurdity of those values that we don't. God is the original satirist. And he has built his comedy on the foundation of his apostles and prophets.

Afterword

In Good Company

I began this story explaining how I was driven by the pursuit of reason into a hunger for ideas and rational certainty but ended in the despair of dehumanized abstraction and an intellectualized faith that lacked imagination. My love of the arts and of creativity ruled my career and my personal interests, but my faith was dominated by rationality. I had been living in a struggle over my soul between reason and imagination—a struggle that originated in the modern scientific rationalistic way of looking at the world taught to me by my culture.

Since becoming aware of this cultural bias with its blessings and curses as well as the Bible's imaginative approach to truth and God, I have continued on my journey to seek a better balance between my intellect and emotions, between my reason and my imagination. But it remains a difficult task. I don't consider myself as having arrived or even living out my revelations as consistently as I would like. Old habits die hard. And doubts remain, accusing me of starting down the slippery slope to heterodoxy, of swinging the pendulum to another extreme, of worshiping images! Or maybe these accusations are just the toxic residue of the unbiblical paradigm of modernism that I've unveiled in my soul and sought to remove.

In light of these uncertainties, it was an amazing encouragement and affirmation to discover quite recently that a personal hero of mine, C. S. Lewis, had not only gone through this same struggle but experienced a similar transformation in his own intellectual and creative life. Apparently Lewis, famous for both his apologetics and his fantasy fiction, had struggled for many years over his imagination and intellect. Author Peter Schakel chronicles this struggle in his book *Reason and Imagination in C. S. Lewis: A Study of "Till We Have Faces."* Lewis's poem "Reason," probably written before he was a Christian, describes his internal tension as an ancient battle between science and mythology, between the so-called clarity of reason and dark obscurity of imagination.[1]

REASON

> Set on the soul's acropolis the reason stands
> A virgin, arm'd, commercing with celestial light,
> And he who sins against her has defiled his own
> Virginity: no cleansing makes his garment white;
> So clear is reason. But how dark, imagining,
> Warm, dark, obscure and infinite, daughter of Night:
> Dark is her brow, the beauty of her eyes with sleep
> Is loaded, and her pains are long, and her delight.
> Tempt not Athene. Wound not in her fertile pains

---

[1] Peter J. Schakel, preface to *Reason and Imagination in C. S. Lewis: A Study of "Till We Have Faces"* (Grand Rapids: Eerdmans, 1984), accessed March 11, 2009, at <http://hope.edu/academic/english/schakel/tillwehavefaces/publishing.html>.

> Demeter, nor rebel against her mother-right.
> Oh who will reconcile in me both maid and mother,
> Who make in me a concord of the depth and height?
> Who make imagination's dim exploring touch
> Ever report the same as intellectual sight?
> Then could I truly say, and not deceive,
> Then wholly say, that I BELIEVE.[2]

At this early point in his life Lewis's love of imagination seemed a contradiction to his highly rational mind. Nevertheless, imagination appeared to touch the infinite in a way that reason could not, and it haunted him.

Lewis had his confidence in the ability of reason to establish the existence of God shaken in a public debate with G. E. M. Anscombe. Apparently, Anscombe's critique was effective in challenging Lewis's privileged status as apologist. Ironically, since Anscombe was a Catholic, she was disagreeing with Lewis not over God's existence but merely on his arguments for God's existence. It was shortly after this incident that Lewis became more focused on writing fiction and less on abstract argumentation.[3]

Michael Ward, writing on the creative genius undergirding the Narnia Chronicles, argues that Lewis's turn to fiction and specifically the "Narniad" was "a deliberate engagement with, rather than a retreat from [Abscombe's] critique of his theology."[4] It wasn't that Lewis ditched the double-sided razor-sharp countours of reason and "fled" to the esoteric safety of ambiguous creative writing. It was more an application of a growing realization of the

---

[2]C. S. Lewis, *Poems* (Orlando: Harcourt, 1964, 1992), p. 81. Quoted in ibid.
[3]Schakel, *Reason and Imagination,* accessed March 11, 2009, at <http://hope.edu/academic/english/schakel/tillwehavefaces/chapter13.html>.
[4]Michael Ward, *Planet Narnia: The Seven Heavens in the Imagination of C. S. Lewis* (New York: Oxford University Press, 2008), p. 4.

danger of an intellectualized faith that he would write about in a later essay:

> I have found that nothing is more dangerous to one's own faith than the work of an apologist. No doctrine of that Faith seems to me so spectral, so unreal as one that I have just successfully defended in a public debate. For a moment, you see, it has seemed to rest on oneself: as a result, when you go away from that debate, it seems no stronger than that weak pillar. That is why we apologists take our lives in our hands and can be saved only by falling back continually from the web of our own arguments, as from our intellectual counters, into the Reality—from Christian apologetics into Christ Himself.[5]

Lewis was pulling away from his unshakable modernist faith in the powers of abstract reason and seeking the uncertain experiential reality of relationship with God. In *A Grief Observed*, Lewis expresses his doubt in the ability of scientific observation—and its finite counterpart the rational intellect—in truly comprehending reality:

> Five senses; an incurably abstract intellect; a haphazardly selective memory; a set of preconceptions and assumptions so numerous that I can never examine more than a minority of them—never become even conscious of them all. How much of total reality can such an apparatus let through?[6]

It would be wrong to conclude that Lewis was swinging the pendulum from an intellectual faith to an anti-intellectual faith.

[5]C. S. Lewis, "Christian Apologetics," in *God in the Dock: Essays on Theology and Ethics*, ed. Walter Hooper (Grand Rapids: Eerdmans, 1970), p. 103.
[6]C. S. Lewis, *A Grief Observed* (New York: HarpeCollins, 1961), p. 64.

More accurately, he was recognizing the limitations of the very organs of knowledge that he had relied upon. Reality was much bigger and more allusive than he had previously so presumptuously assumed. And it was imagination that he had previously considered "dark and obscure" that was actually able to access reality in ways reason could only dream of. The battle in his soul was turning in favor of imagination. Quoting a letter from Lewis to a literature society in the last years of his life, Schakel illustrates Lewis's journey and revelation of the superiority of imagination in his spiritual literary endeavors:

> The imaginative man in me is older, more continuously operative, and in that sense more basic than either the religious writer or the critic. It was he who made me first attempt (with little success) to be a poet. It was he who, in response to the poetry of others, made me a critic, and, in defence of that response, sometimes a critical controversialist. It was he who after my conversion led me to embody my religious belief in symbolical or mythopeic forms, ranging from *Screwtape* to a kind of theologised science fiction. And it was of course he who has brought me, in the last few years, to write the series of Narnian stories for children; not asking what children want and then endeavouring to adapt myself (this was not needed) but because the fairy tale was the genre best fitted for what I wanted to say.[7]

Lewis went from being an imaginative youth, to a rational adult who subordinated imagination to reason, to a writer who tried to integrate his imagination rationally, to an artist who re-

---

[7]Letter from C. S. Lewis, quoted in Schakel, *Reason and Imagination*, accessed March 11, 2009, at <http://hope.edu/academic/english/schakel/tillwehavefaces/chapter13.html>.

turned to his youthful imagination. Like Jesus telling parables, Lewis came to believe that some aspects of truth, reality and God can only be captured through stories of the imagination.

Lewis's worship and awe of God's majesty through the powers of imagination in a universe of images can perhaps be best expressed through imaginative prose. Here Ransom, the protagonist of his novel *Perelandra,* looks out on the night sky and muses on his own enlightenment of freedom from the deadness of Enlightenment science and reason:

> A nightmare, long engendered in the modern mind by the mythology that follows in the wake of science, was falling off him. He had read of "Space": at the back of his thinking for years had lurked the dismal fancy of the black, cold vacuity, the utter deadness, which was supposed to separate the worlds . . . but now that very name "Space" seemed a blasphemous libel for this empyrean ocean of radiance in which they swam. He could not call it "dead"; he felt life pouring into him from it every moment. How indeed should it be otherwise, since out of this ocean the worlds and all their life had come? He had thought it barren: he saw now that it was the womb of worlds. No: space was the wrong name. Older thinkers had been wiser when they named it simply the heavens—the heavens which declared the glory—the
> "happy climes that ly
> Where day never shuts his eye
> Up in the broad fields of the sky."[8]

What Lewis had learned, what I am learning, at the outer limits of our engagement with Christian faith through reason alone,

---

[8]C. S. Lewis, *Out of the Silent Planet* (New York: Scribner, 2003), p. 34.

is good news: God is bigger than rationality, bigger than imagination, and he is Lord of both. His invitation through Isaiah still rings true as we move gradually from the Age of Reason to the Media Age and as we oscillate back and forth between these paradoxical priorities of word and image:

> "Come now, let us reason together,"
> says the LORD.
> "Though your sins are like scarlet,
> they shall be as white as snow;
> though they are red as crimson,
> they shall be like wool." (Is 1:18)

Appendix

Answering Objections

Word-oriented Christians often react with hostility to the suggestion that image is just as legitimate a means to the God of communication as word is. They cannot conceive that a movie or a painting can possibly have as much value or influence as a preached sermon or written systematic theology. Some decry the rise of the image and the fall of the word in our culture and lament for "better days" when print culture ruled the day and image was "in its place" as a subordinate and mistrusted medium. They are concerned about the negative effects on civilization that image brings. And they have some good arguments, arguments that I would like to explore in this appendix. I'll subtitle the arguments, spell them out briefly, and try to answer them equally as brief.

WORDS ARE INVISIBLE LIKE SPIRIT; IMAGES ARE VISIBLE LIKE THE FLESH

Many people assume that "image" refers only to things that are visible and "word" refers only to abstractions—things that are, in effect, "invisible." For ease of reference, I will refer to this dichotomy as the "visible/invisible fallacy." But as I explained from the start,

we are talking about the *categories* of rationality (word) and imagination (image).

Visual images and printed words both affect the way we think and perceive the world. Many communications theorists agree that the dominance of the printed word has produced a certain kind of abstract thinking.[1] But as author Mitchell Stevens notes, written words' great limitation grows out of this great strength of abstraction. He writes that writing

is a system of representation, or code, that represents another system of representation, another code: spoken language. The written word *face*—to oversimplify a bit—calls to mind the sound "*fās*." It is, therefore, two steps removed from that expressive skin sculpture itself. . . . Increasingly in the five thousand years since the development of writing, [our eyes] have been reduced to staring at letters of identical size and color, arranged in lines of identical length, on pages of identical size and color. Readers, in a sense, are no longer asked to see; they are simply asked to interpret the code.[2]

The category of visible and invisible are not so exclusive to image and word as some think. Consider the visual nature of words. If you look at the picture in figure 9.1 (p. 193), what do you see? You see the image of a shepherd.

Again, what do you see in figure 9.2 (p. 193)? You see a shepherd.

---

[1]Mitchell Stevens, *the rise of the image the fall of the word* (New York: Oxford University Press, 1998), pp. 20-21.
[2]Ibid., pp. 63-64.

Figure 9.1. What do you see?

A SHEPHERD

Figure 9.2. What do you see?

The first figure (the image) is representational, the second figure (the word) is symbolic. Technically, written words are just as much images as any painting or other visual image. The main difference is that they are symbolic as opposed to representational. So, in a way, the privileging of written words over visual images is really the privileging of one kind of image (symbolic) over another kind of image (representational).

But aren't mental images different from physical images? Yes, they are different, but not so different as some would like to assert. When you see a visual picture of a shepherd, you are viewing an external public image. But when you read the word *shepherd,* you merely displace the *location* of the image from external and public to internal and private. You are privileging mental visual images over physical visual images. Thus a Scripture like Psalm 89:13, "God has a strong right arm," is rightly considered imagery because it is a "word-picture," words that paint a picture in the mind rather than appeal to some kind of abstract reasoning.

Sometimes words are invisible, as in speech, sometimes they are visible images, as in written words. Sometimes imagery is visible as in visual pictures, sometimes it is invisible, in the mind. Imagery can involve more empirical senses than the eye, such as a  movie, but word also involves the eye in reading, or the ear in hearing, and in that way has a sensate aspect to it.

This is not to say, however, that words are merely reducible to images. For much of imagination involves words, reason and propositions as well. For example, a story about Moses includes propositions about his life or what God has said. When we talk about a painting or a movie, we use analytical discourse in our interaction with the medium. A musical composition follows an underlying rational structure of order. Words and images are not reducible to each other, they are interdependent concepts that can be distinguished but not always separated.

THIS BOOK IS WRITTEN IN RATIONAL PROPOSITIONAL WORDS

This very book, arguing as it does for assigning a high value to imagery, is itself predominantly rational and propositional in method. Doesn't that seem like a contradiction?

Not at all. The Bible values words, books, rationality, propositions and logic, and therefore, so do I. I am not suggesting in the least that we scrap words and rationality because of the failure of modernity to measure up to biblical balance. Nor am I suggesting a pendulum swing of the superiority of image over word. I am suggesting that image has been devalued, thus we are impoverished in our biblical understanding of truth *and* God, and we need to have an equal ultimacy of both word *and* image in our cultural vocabulary.

I have been engaged in visual and dramatic imagery as an artist for many years. The fact that I also write propositional words reinforces my call to unity of engaging in both. We must have sermons and rational argumentation, but we must also have story, drama and other tactile imagery in our theological exploration of God or we miss God's fullness.

GOD LEFT US NO CANONICAL WORKS OF ART

Some might argue that God gave us only words in the Scripture, not pieces of art. If God considered images or art to be as valid as words, he would have left us with some. Since he did not, then imagery must not be as important as words.

This entire book has been a verification that the Bible itself is a work of art. The nature of narrative, parables, verbal imagery, metaphors and stories of visions, miracles and dreams is precisely a literary *art form* and not a scientific or rationalistic discourse. Just because it is written in words does not negate its artistic nature and does not reduce it to logocentricity.

If God used image to reveal himself and truth (such as in dreams and visions), then image is *not* a second-class means of communication. It's just as important a part of the process. Second Timothy 3:16 says that "all Scripture is inspired by God," or "God-breathed" words. But does this mean that the images, visions and dreams that God gave were not also "God-breathed"? Of course not. Both images *and* words are God's "Word," or as we indicated earlier, God's message. A person's testimony of what God has done in their life is not more important than what God actually did in their life.

Biblical apologists defend the inerrancy of Scripture by appealing to the "original autographs" as being without flaw, as opposed to the copies or translations that we have.[3] In a similar sense the written words are the translation of the experience or original vision from God. So the biblical legitimacy of the final written words does not eliminate the biblical legitimacy of the images upon which they are based. Both word and image are equally God-breathed communication. To pit one against the other is to pit God's Word against God's Word.

It is true that without words, we could not have the Bible as we now have it. But it is equally true that without dreams, visions, and other incarnate *imagery*, we could not have the Bible as we now have it. God's use of words surely legitimates words as a sufficient, but not exhaustive, means of communication. In the same way, his use of images surely legitimates imagery as a sufficient, but not exhaustive, means of communication.

---

[3]This strikes me as a questionable procedure: Attempting to prove the perfection of something that we do not have. I can understand this as a faith commitment, but not an evidential proof.

IMAGES NEED WORDS,
WORDS DON'T NEED IMAGES

Words, it is argued, can instruct without images, but images must be interpreted with words or they are arbitrary or unknowable. In this view image is subordinate to word. God's visions and dreams all had to be interpreted with words. If they did not, then they would be meaningless or confusing, with a hundred different possible interpreta-  tions. The prophet walking around naked without explanation would be no different than a lewd criminal streaking through the city. Words give meaning, images confuse or are too ambiguous.

Considering the vast amount of imagery we have already shown to be the foundation of God's revelation, however, is it not unbiblical speculation to argue that God *could have* communicated his truth in words alone without images, or for that matter, in images alone without words? The fact is, he didn't choose words alone. And if he didn't, then that should cause us to be cautious about suggesting that one of God's chosen means of communication (image) is inferior to another (word).

Meanwhile, any perusal of a dictionary will illustrate that words often have dozens of shades of differing potential meanings. As Mitchell Stevens points out, "Writers can never be sure that their words have only one possible interpretation. As our literary theorists have spent a third of a century pointing out, readers bring different experiences and interests to the sentences they read and therefore take different meanings from them."[4]

---

[4]Stevens, *rise of the image*, p. 67.

Words are often just as confusing or unclear as images.

Words are inescapable, true enough. But it is also true that images are inescapable. Many biblical concepts cannot be described in mere words of abstraction without imagery. Take for instance, the kingdom of God. Jesus almost exclusively used parables for the kingdom because of the inadequacy of abstract rationality alone to convey it. The Old Testament also uses images—allegorical, symbolical and metaphorical—to express the kingdom of God: wolves and lambs grazing together (Is 65), nations streaming to a mountain (Is 2; 11) that grows and fills the earth (Dan 2), an uncrossable river (Ezek 47:1-12). Without words of explanation what would biblical images mean? But without incarnate images and experiences from God, what would the biblical authors have to say? Abstract rational propositions of the eternal truths of reason? No way. Language is necessary to our identity as human beings created in the image of God, but God did not create us as disembodied intellects. Language has many forms; spoken, written, or imaged, abstract or concrete. Blessed is he who uses all those forms as much as possible.

IMAGES MANIPULATE EMOTIONS

Another criticism of image as a legitimate means of communication

 and persuasion is that images are more emotion-driven than words. People are manipulated because their rational faculties are diverted with the nature of image-oriented mediums. We've all complained about how advertising manipulates people to buy things they don't want or need. We've complained how the techniques of filmmaking and television news bypass rationality and form attitudes in people by selective visuals, out-of-context presentations or outright visual fabrication.

In his book *The Vanishing Word*, Arthur Hunt makes the argument that an image-orientation in our culture disarms our analytical and critical faculties. It diffuses our "mental defenses to arm ourselves against demagoguery" and makes us more susceptible to tyranny. It supplants the idea of Christianity as a religion of the book.[5] No doubt these dangers are real for imagocentrism. But they are also real dangers of logocentrism as well. Mormons, Jehovah's Witnesses and Muslims are word-oriented "people of the book," yet many nonetheless ignorantly follow demagogues and tyrants like lemmings into the sea. Books, words and reading haven't rescued them from their ignorance, they have reinforced it. Word has the same potential for good or bad as image does.

Images cut out of context can make lies look like truth or visually connect opposing ideas as if they were consistent. So for instance, a news story about the war on terrorism followed by a series of commercials about toothpaste and soda will tend to trivialize the importance of the war as just another product being sold. The old Nazi propaganda trick of dissolving images of rats into images of Jews carries the same sort of deception of image. Neil Postman, in his classic *Amusing Ourselves to Death*, laments the modern inability to detect lies because of the fragmentary nature and soundbite editing of television news visuals.[6] This potential of image toward irrationality and contradiction is certainly a valid concern. But yet again, this concern can be equally applied to word and rational discourse itself. Postman himself uses newspapers—*word-oriented communications*—as an example of soundbites

---

[5]Arthur W. Hunt III, *The Vanishing Word: The Veneration of Visual Imagery in the Postmodern World* (Wheaton, Ill.: Crossway Books, 2003), pp. 25, 213-40.
[6]Neil Postman, *Amusing Ourselves to Death: Public Discourse in the Age of Show Business* (New York: Penguin Books, 1985), pp. 107-13.

and fragmentation, thus affirming the manipulative power of the word. Words often promote irrationality (Friedrich Nietzsche's books) and regularly manipulate emotions (sermons of politicians and TV evangelists). The image rhetoric of Joseph Goebbels's propaganda were no more manipulative than the logical rhetoric of Hitler's book *Mein Kampf* or his sermonic oration. Michael Moore's films are no more logically or emotionally manipulative than his books. The problem is not so much with the medium being manipulative as it is with people being manipulative with whatever medium they use to communicate.

It is important to note that in ancient times, the change from a verbal culture to a written culture was attended with the same exact fears that moderns now have of the change from a word culture to an image culture. Plato writes of the Egyptian king Thamus bemoaning the perils of written words being the same as the peril of painting pictures, in that there is a lazy submission of man's mind to the form of written words:

> This discovery of yours [written words] will create forget-fulness in the learners' souls, because they will not use their memories; they will trust to the external written characters and not remember of themselves . . . you give your disciples not truth, but only the semblance of truth; they will be hearers of many things and will have learned nothing; they will appear to be omniscient and will generally know noth-ing; they will be tiresome company, having the show of wisdom without the reality.[7]

---

[7]Plato *Phaedrus* 275, in *Great Books of the Western World* (Chicago: Encyclopaedia Britannica, 1971, 6:138-39.

With the invention of the Western printing press in the sixteenth century and subsequent mass production of written words, critics mouthed the same exact concerns about written words that are now exclaimed of moving images: that printed words would "scatter prejudice and ignorance through a people," that the dissemination of printed matter would be the "most powerful of ignorance's weapons," that eighteenth-century newspapers reduced politics to acting and facts to soundbites, that books were mindlessly addictive and left the reader with an emptiness of soul. Such critiques came from learned men like Alexander Pope, Leo Tolstoy and Ralph Waldo Emerson.[8] In many ways, these men's fears were proven correct. The printed word has spread ignorance, prejudice and irrationality, just as much as it has spread literacy, education and rationality.

In the 1960s, the era when Marshall McLuhan began warning us of the medium being the message and all the worry warts were fearing the dumbing down nature of visual communications like television, Edmund Carpenter reversed the charges against reading:

> When we read, another person thinks for us: we merely repeat his mental process. The greater part of the work of thought is done for us. This is why it relieves us to take up a book after being occupied by our own thoughts. In reading, the mind is only the playground for another's ideas. People who spend most of their lives in reading often lose the ca-

[8]Stevens, *rise of the image*, pp. 34-36.

pacity for thinking, just as those who always ride forget how to walk. Some people read themselves stupid.[9]

With all the dangers of image-worship in our culture toward emotional manipulation and irrationality, there is just as much danger of word-worship toward emotional manipulation and irrationality *as well as* intellectual manipulation and dehumanization.

In fact, one could argue that more damage has been done to humanity in the twentieth century alone, through the manipulative words of Karl Marx, Charles Darwin, Sigmund Freud and Friedrich Nietzsche, than all the ancient image cultures combined.

IMAGES DISTORT REALITY THROUGH ILLUSION

Image-orientation is accused of distorting reality through artifice. As author Richard Lints complains, storytelling is a questionable "vinyl narrative" of unintended consequences because

it is an artificial medium whose primary intent is to amuse. Its hidden assumption is that the world unfolds before the audience as the human author imagined it. Its message is that the world can be like this if you want it to be. . . . Drama is a medium that reinforces the artificial character of truth.[10]

---

[9]Edmund Carpenter, "The New Languages," in *Mass Media: Forces in Our Society*, 2nd ed., ed. Voelker (New York: Harcourt, Brace Jovanovich, 1975), pp. 373-74. Thanks to Azusa Pacific University communications professor John Hamilton for this reference.
[10]Richard Lints, "The Vinyl Narratives: The Metanarrative of Postmodernity and the Recovery of a Churchly Theology," in *A Confessing Theology for Postmodern Times*, ed. Michael Horton (Wheaton, Ill.: Crossway Books, 2000), p. 95.

This criticism has a long and distinguished history, from Plato's concern about painted pictures deceiving through the "imitation of appearance" over "real things," all the way through historian Daniel Boorstin's 1962 prophetic book *The Image*, declaring images as the "menace of unreality."

But this is another case where the same danger is inherent in word-orientation. Writing uses the same techniques of selectivity (as in Charles Darwin's writing), pulling out of context (as with Karl Marx), and outright lying (as with notorious cases from such trustworthy names as the *New York Times* and veteran news anchor Dan Rather) that Lints is concerned about regarding images. Words distort reality through artifice, assume that the world "unfolds as the human author imagined it" and "reinforce the artificial character of truth." Just read any book by the titans of modernity and you'll get a five-course meal of the "menace of unreality" and artificial pictures of the world they paint with their words. As stated earlier, the twentieth century is littered with a hundred million corpses and millions of eternally damned souls due to the "unintended consequences" of words, books and propositions of these word-oriented thinkers and movements.

One Christian cultural critic says the following in criticizing image used in television:

> For television, any real truth is impossible. . . . The viewer
> does not see the event. He sees . . . an edited image of that

event, one that gives an illusion of objectivity and truth…
with television, reality becomes the image, "whether or not
that image corresponds to any objective state of affairs—
and we are not challenged to engage in this analysis."[11]

Replace every "television" with "book" and every "image"
with "word" and you will see how the charges against images are
equally chargeable against words. It's just simply not true that
words and books are less distorting or illusory than images and
multimedia. The medium is not necessarily the message, but the
message often abuses the medium.

WORD CULTURES IMPROVE, IMAGE CULTURES DECLINE

Arthur Hunt claims that word-based
movements like the Protestant Reformation, Puritanism and the founding
American experiment emphasized literacy, which led to moral and civil
achievement.[12] He contrasts these with
the ancient pagan cultures that he
claims were image-based, like ancient
Egypt, Greece and Rome, which led to
unrestrained chaos. He quotes a well-
known anthropological maxim, "As
language distinguishes man from ani-
mal, so writing distinguishes civilized man from the barbarian."[13]

[11]Mark Earley, "CNN's Snuff Film: Appalling Hypocrisy," *This Week's Viewpoint*,
    October 26, 2006, accessed February 5, 2008, at <www.crownvideo.com/viewpoint/
    index.cfm?Price=USprice>.
[12]Hunt, *Vanishing Word,* pp. 26-52.
[13]Ibid., p. 37.

While I would agree with the superiority of the three former cultures over the three latter, such oversimplification is certainly unwarranted. The success or failure of the cultures is based not on their being word- or image-centered but in the totality of their worldviews. On his criteria, one could argue that the absolutist nature of rationality-oriented, logocentric cultures fostered the inflexibility and intolerance that led to wars such as the Thirty Years' War, which developed out of the Reformation. Under the wonderful logocentric American experiment, rationalistic doctors murder millions of preborn children a year by cutting them into pieces, burning their flesh off with salt and chemicals, and sucking their brains out with vacuums.

Meanwhile, ancient Greeks worshiped rationality and the word! Logocentrism is practically their invention. Or consider the Hebrew culture, ignored in Hunt's list. In this very book I've shown just how saturated in image and sensual experience their religion was. The difference was in the content of their sensate celebration, not in the form or style of it. The difference between sinful celebration and godly celebration, is not in using imagery or words, but in what deity the imagery and words are used for.

The idea that "writing distinguishes man from the barbarian" is another modern vestige of the Enlightenment lie that education is salvation. History shows in fact that writing has not always made men less barbaric, but it has made barbarians more effective in their barbarism, and enabled them to spread ignorance more widely. Writing, education and knowledge helped Nazis be more efficient in killing Jews with more effective machines. Writing helped Soviet Communists for eighty-nine years to more effectively propagandize their people into complete ignorance of reality.

The fact is, literacy can and does spread civilization. But it also spreads evil and barbarism as well. And it does so just as easily if not more so than imagery.

IMAGE CREATES THE CULT OF CELEBRITY

Another complaint that Hunt raises against image-oriented culture is its tendency to worship celebrity. Because images become iconographic in nature through mass media, including the larger-than-life persona of entertainment, celebrity has raged in the twentieth century.[14]

Hunt unwittingly reveals later, however, that word-oriented culture suffers *from the same exact celebrity worship as do image-oriented ones.* He quotes a journalist's remarks, "Where we once deified the lifestyles of writers such as Hemingway and F. Scott Fitzgerald, we now fantasize about rock-and-roll gods, movie starlets or NBA superstuds. The notion of writer-as-culture-hero is dead and gone."[15] What is so ironic about this quote is that the lives of Hemingway and Fitzgerald were not in essence any different than rock gods and movie stars. They were easily as debauched and intellectually opposed to God as most Hollywood celebrities today. And just like Hollywood celebrities, they were exalted for their talent, not their character.

The truth is, from the beginning of creation, man has suffered the sin of celebrity worship. Sometimes those celebrities are men

---

[14]Ibid., pp. 173-76.
[15]Ibid., p. 195.

of both words and images, like emperors or rulers; sometimes they are men of books and words, like Plato and Aristotle, who had entire schools following their every utterance; sometimes they are men of empirical sciences; sometimes they are men of image without substance like politicians and pretty people. But at the end of the day, the cult of celebrity is fueled in both image and word-oriented cultures.

IMAGE CULTIVATES SENSUALITY

A corollary closely linked to emotion is sensuality. As Hunt argues, images are seductive because they are physical. He claims an image-saturated society is deeply connected to pagan sensuality. The evidence of course is our own media-saturated pagan world filled with sexually explicit and violent exploitation from MTV rock videos to movies and magazines.[16]

In one sense, he is right. Much of our imagery is pagan in its sensuality, and this should cause alarm—just as alarm should be caused by the pagan-influenced, word-oriented academic journals, university departments, purveyors of scientism and modernist preachers. Alarm should be raised by the increase of *books* full of pagan ideas that reach the masses as well as the educational, political and media elite. Words can be just as sensually pagan as images.

The Marquis de Sade (1740-1814) wrote during the Enlighten-

---

[16]Ibid., pp. 29-52.

ment, the word-oriented culture that spawned modernity. And yet, the depraved sensuality in his *books of words* could make the publishers of Penthouse Images blush. He describes grotesque sexual fantasies of sado-masochism, rape, mutilation and murder that rival any modern cult horror film. And he did it in a logo-centric era.